SPORTS QUOTES AND ANECDOTES

by

Robert Harrison

DORRANCE PUBLISHING CO., INC.
PITTSBURGH, PENNSYLVANIA 15222

ISBN #0-8059-4110-X
Printed in the United States of America

First Printing

For information or to order additional books, please write:
Dorrance Publishing Co., Inc.
643 Smithfield Street
Pittsburgh, Pennsylvania 15222
U.S.A.

This book is dedicated to all good sports who comply with the request of the late Jim Britt, play-by-play announcer for the Boston Red Sox, who closed each broadcast with, "...and remember, if you can't take part in a sport, be one anyway, will ya?"

SPORTS QUOTES AND ANECDOTES

INTRODUCTION

WHY HUMOROUS *SPORTS QUOTES AND ANECDOTES?*

During the summer between my junior and senior college years, I had the opportunity of playing in a summer league consisting of six teams, comprised of above-average college baseball players from all sections of the country. It was a highly enjoyable experience, highlighted by many amusing incidents, one of which I would like to share with you.

Our team held a comfortable 12–2 lead in the late innings, behind a fine pitching performance by our rather eccentric but talented left-handed pitcher. Bored with the futile efforts of the opposing hitters and two strikes on the batter, "Lefty" picked up the resin bag, nonchalantly bounced it around in his hand, and bent over to place it on the ground behind the pitching mound. Instead he placed the baseball on the ground and retained the resin bag. Swinging into his long, graceful, left-hand windup, he threw the bag toward the plate. The batter swung mightily and hit a short pop fly halfway between the pitching mound and home plate. Our catcher whipped off his mask and pounced on the "ball" as it struck the ground. Playing first base, I moved over to the first base bag anticipating the catcher's throw for the putout. To my great surprise, our catcher, after drawing his arm back to make the throw, obviously felt the resin bag crush in this hand and simply tossed it to the plate umpire. The hitter, meanwhile, was crossing first base believing he had beat out an infield hit.

The crowd roared with laughter when word quickly spread that our pitcher had thrown the resin bag. That roar remained in my ears and mind for months after the incident. I knew there had to be many other amusing incidents at sporting events that precipitated statements or comments by the participants so I commenced cataloging such incidents, knowing how much people enjoyed the lighter side of sporting events.

While Americans are perhaps the most knowledgeable and rabid sports fans, we have historically always enjoyed the humorous side. I hope you will find these amusing sports quotes and anecdotes entertaining and enjoyable. I hope they will also remind you of similar events in which you had been a participant or a spectator.

For more than fifteen years, I have compiled and cataloged the contents from newspapers and magazines. These quotes are exactly the way I found them in print and are presented for your enjoyment.

Robert Harrison
Osterville,
Massachusetts

PART 1

BASEBALL

A Brief History

Baseball, a competitive athletic game of skill, is universally regarded as the American national sport. In addition to being the most popular game in the United States, baseball is played by a multitude of amateurs, representing numerous "sand lot" clubs; athletic associations; and virtually every high school, preparatory school, and college in the country.

By the end of the eighteenth century, several primitive varieties of baseball were played in the United States. Most of these early variations were played with stakes marking the "stations." Since these resulted in injuries, stones were substituted about 1840. Then sand-filled sacks called bases were used, hence the name baseball.

In 1845 the foundation of modern baseball was created when the Knickerbocker Club was organized in New York City. On June 19, 1846, this team played its first game in Hoboken, New Jersey, against the New York Nine. Professional baseball began in 1869 by the Cincinnati Red Stockings. In 1871 the National Association of Professional Baseball Players was organized with clubs in Boston, Philadelphia, Chicago, Brooklyn, New York, Cleveland, and four other cities.

The Baseball Hall of Fame, opened in 1939 in Cooperstown, New York, has information about the history of the sport as well as a wealth of memorabilia, such as uniforms, photographs, and trophies.

SPORTS QUOTES AND ANECDOTES
BASEBALL

In the late innings of a particularly close and hard fought game, Baltimore Orioles' second baseman **BILLY RIPKEN** was ejected by plate umpire **TERRY COONEY** for tossing his helmet. Orioles manager **FRANK ROBINSON** rushed out of the dugout to talk with Cooney.

"I was the peacemaker. I asked why Ripkin was thrown out of the game.

"'Well, he took his helmet off his head!' said the empire.

"'Of course he took off his helmet, he wasn't going to throw it with his head in it, was he?'"

JIM ROOKER, former Pittsburgh Pirates' pitcher, on manager **CHUCK TANNER**: "He used to have a bed check just for me every night. No problem. The bed was always there."

RAY DANDRIDGE, the Negro League star inducted into baseball's Hall of Fame, was delighted to see **WILLIE MAYS** make it to the big leagues.

"I recall playing with Mays at Minneapolis of the American Association. I was hitting behind Willie, which became a problem. Every time Willie would hit a home run, the opposing pitcher would knock me down on the first pitch. Finally I went to our team manager and said, 'Skip, if you don't get that man out from hitting ahead of me, I'm gonna get killed!'"

BOB UECKER, former Major League catcher and humorist: "The highlight of my baseball career came in Philadelphia's **CONNIE MACK** Stadium, when I saw a fan fall out of the upper deck. When he got up and walked away, the crowed booed."

ANDY VAN SLYKE of the Pittsburgh Pirates, on salary gripes of fellow ballplayers: "Every single ballplayer should have to work at a Chrysler or General Motors plant to see just what we have in baseball."

When the New York Mets were selecting players in the 1962 National League expansion draft, Mets manager **CASEY STENGEL** plucked catcher **HOBIE LANDRITH** from the San Francisco Giants as his first pick. When asked why, Casey answered matter-of-factly: "You gotta start with a catcher, because if you don't, you'll have all passed balls."

In 1979 **MIKE FLANAGAN**, Baltimore Orioles star left-hand pitcher, dispelled any rumors of his being involved in any trade with the New York Yankees. Said Flanagan: "I could never play in New York. I can remember the first time I was called in from the bullpen to relieve our starting pitcher. As I got into the bullpen cart (for the ride to the pitcher's mound), the cart driver told me to be sure and lock the doors."

Former White Sox slugging star, first baseman **DICK ALLEN**, expressing his dislike of synthetic baseball fields: "If a horse can't eat it, I don't want to play on it."

A Minnesota Twins official, on learning that the trade that brought pitcher **JOHN SMILEY** from the Pittsburgh Pirates included $860,000 to help pay Smiley's $3.44 million salary, said in disgust: "It's like robbing a bank and having the police drive you home."

New York Yankee catcher **YOGI BERRA**: "Your home opening game is always a great day, especially if you're not on the road."

Former Cardinals third baseman **MIKE SHANNON** on Dodgers' pitcher **DON DRYSDALE**: "Don Drysdale would consider an intentional walk a waste of three pitches. If he wants to put you on base, he will hit you with the first one."

Los Angeles Dodgers first baseman **KAL DANIELS**, after the Atlanta Braves' **DEION SANDERS**, All-Pro cornerback with the Atlanta Falcons football team, ran over Daniels at first base: "I think we need some yard markers out here."

Former Cincinnati Reds baseball great **PETE ROSE**: "Doctors tell me I have the body of a thirty-year-old. I know I have the brain of a fifteen-year-old. If you've got both, you can play baseball."

Author **GEORGE V. HIGGINS**: "In Boston we believe, and we are never disappointed because what we believe is this: The world will break your heart someday, but we are luckier than most—we get ours broken by the Red Sox every year, at Fenway Park."

MEL HALL, former Cleveland Indians outfielder, who had gone homerless all season at Cleveland Stadium, promised he'd do something special for the fans when he hit his first. When he finally did hit one, it turned out to be an inside-the-park homer, and he said: "I didn't have time to do my cabbage-patch dance." Said Cleveland manager **DOC EDWARDS**; "It's a good thing, or I would have turned him into coleslaw."

New York Yankees Hall of Fame pitcher **LEFTY GOMEZ**: "The secret of my success was clean living and fast outfielders."

Former New York Giants manager **LEO DUROCHER**: "If somebody came up and hit .450, stole 100 bases, and performed a miracle in the field everyday, I'd still look you in the eye and say **WILLIE MAYS** was better. He could do the five things you have to do to be a superstar: Hit, hit with power, run, throw, and field. And he had that other magic ingredient that turns a superstar into a super superstar. He lit up the room when he came in. He was a joy to be around."

Former Los Angeles Dodgers star southpaw and Hall of Fame pitcher **SANDY KOUFAX**: "I became a good pitcher when I stopped trying to make the hitters miss the ball and started trying to make them hit it."

BILL DICKEY, New York Yankee catcher, went out to the mound to talk with pitcher **LEFTY GOMEZ** on how to pitch to the next batter, Red Sox slugger **JIMMIE FOXX**: "What do you want to throw him?" he asked. "I don't want to throw him nothin'," said Gomez, eyeing Foxx nervously. "Maybe he'll just get tired of waiting and head back to the dugout."

From former baseball great and humorist **CASEY STENGEL**:
"Going to bed with a woman never hurt a ball player. It's staying up all night looking for them that does you in."
"Good pitching will always stop good hitting and vice versa."
"Managing is getting paid for home runs someone else hits."
"Whenever I decided to release a guy, I always had his room searched first for a gun. You couldn't take chances with some of those birds."
Asked how he was feeling, "Not bad. Most people my age are dead. You could look it up."
"Show me a good loser and I'll show you a loser,"
After his New York Mets ended a seventeen-game losing streak, "Whew, I thought we would have to call in the fire department my team's so hot."

Baltimore Oriole coach **FRANK ROBINSON** in the clubhouse after a game in which the Toronto Blue Jays hit ten home runs that seemed to have the Oriole outfielders looking up at the sky all afternoon, following the flight of the baseballs going over the fences: "Okay, all the outfielders into the training room for a neck rub."

Baltimore manager **EARL WEAVER**:
"In order to keep doing what we've done, we have to keep doing what we've done in the past."

"It's what you learn after you know it all that counts."

"You can be smart and be a dumb player or be dumb and be a smart player but the player or manager who does best is someone with good baseball judgment."

"I never got many questions about my managing. I tried to get twenty-five guys who didn't ask questions."

CLARK GRIFFITH, owner of the Minnesota Twins: "Before the season started, we took a survey of the fans and found out they wanted to see home runs more than anything else. So we went out to build a pitching staff to oblige them."

American League umpire **RON LUCIANO**: "When I started in baseball, it was played by nine tough competitors on grass, in the daylight, in graceful ballparks. By the time I was finished, there were ten men on each side, the game was played indoors, at night, on plastic, and I had to spend half of my time watching out for a man dressed in a chicken suit who kept trying to kiss me."

In a column about baseball great, **YOGI BERRA,** Tony Kornheiser of the *Washington Post* recalled when the New York Yankee catcher was a guest on a radio talk show. Before the show, the host said, "Yogi, if you don't mind, I'd like to play 'Free Association' with you on the air. I'll say a name and you say the first thing that comes to your mind. Okay?"

"Okay," said Yogi.

The show started and the host said, "We've got Yogi Berra of the New York Yankees here, and he and I are going to do some free associating. I'm going to say a name, and Yogi's going to say the first thing that pops into his mind."

After a slight pause, the host said, "**MICKEY MANTLE**," and Yogi quickly replied, "What about him?"

Philadelphia Phillies Hall of Fame pitcher **ROBIN ROBERTS**, when asked his greatest All-Star game thrill: "When **MICKEY MANTLE** bunted with the wind blowing out at Cincinnati's Crosley Field."

CHARLIE LAU, late Chicago White Sox batting coach: "There are two theories on hitting the knuckle ball. Unfortunately neither of them works."

New York Yankee catcher **YOGI BERRA** gave his old pitching pal, **WHITEY FORD**, this scouting report on the New York Mets' spring training complex and the city of Port Lucie, Florida: "They've got six fields and two bars."

Right-handed pitcher **DON SUTTON** after Los Angeles Dodger manager **TOM LASORDA** told him to hang in there when he was getting hit hard during his first pitching term with the Dodgers: "I've got to. I can't sing or dance, and we've already got a pitching coach."

LEFTY GOMEZ, New York Yankees pitcher, to first baseman **LOU GEHRIG** after illness forced Gehrig out of the lineup: "It took fifteen years to get you out of a game. Sometimes I'm out in fifteen minutes."

Said **PHILIP K. WRIGLEY**, chewing gum heir and Chicago Cubs owner: "Baseball is too much of a business to be called a sport and too much of a sport to be called a business."

TOM PACIOREK, Seattle left fielder, after striking out on three pitches against the New York Yankees' star left-hander, **RON GUIDRY**: "Of what I saw of him, he was unhitable, unbeatable, and unthinkable. I might have been more impressed if I had seen more of his stuff."

As a lark, four Los Angeles Kings hockey players took batting practice before a California Angels game at Anaheim Stadium. Afterward one of them said, "I didn't realize the fences were that far away." Replied Angel pitcher **JOHN FARRELL**, who has allowed a club record-high homers: "They're not."

Pittsburgh Pirate star **WILLIE STARGELL**, told that his teammate **DAVE PARKER** had called him his idol: "That's pretty good, considering that Dave's previous idol was himself."

LEE MACPHAIL, American League president, recounting a meeting with Baltimore manager **EARL WEAVER**, whom he subsequently suspended for three games for abusing umpires: "Earl gave me his version of what happened and asked me not to suspend the umpires."

Los Angeles Dodger pitcher **BRIAN HOLTON**, after pitching a night game: "That's the most nervous I've ever been in my life. I was so nervous, I started singing to myself. I was singing, 'You Take the High Road and I'll Take the Low Road,' and I don't even know the words."

When the Atlanta Braves' **DALE MURPHY**, one of the National League's hitting stars, batting .223 at the time, was told he had been voted "Mr. Nice Guy" in an NBC poll, he said: "Who voted, the National League pitchers?"

GEORGE FOSTER, Cincinnati Reds batting star, on word that the Phillies' lumbering outfielder **GREG LUZINSKI** led the league one season by getting hit ten times: "Was that in the field or at the plate?"

STEVE McCATTY, Oakland A's pitcher, after yielding a 450-foot home run to Seattle's **BRUCE BOCHTE**: "Some of our guys would have to pick the ball up and hit it three times to get it that far."

After the first six or seven pitches thrown by Minnesota Twins starting pitcher **PETE REDFERN**, it appeared obvious he simply didn't have his good "stuff." Asked why he let Redfern struggle for more than four innings before yanking him, Minnesota Twins' manager **GENE MAUCH** replied: "I was afraid I might strangle him if I had him in the dugout."

Boston Red Sox pitcher **JOE SAMBITO** on what it takes to sit in the bleachers at Fenway Park: "First, you have to flunk an I.Q. test. Second, you have to be able to drink a gallon of beer. If you can drink more than a gallon, they give you a seat in the front row behind the Red Sox bullpen."

CLINT HURDLE, Kansas City Royals outfielder, who came into baseball as a much-ballyhooed "phenom": "If I had done everything I was supposed to, I would be leading the league in home runs, have the highest batting average, have given $1,000 to the cancer fund, and married Marie Osmond."

DARRELL JOHNSON, former Seattle Mariner manager, on how he knows when it's time to change pitchers: "You just listen to the bat and the ball come together. They make an awful noise."

When short stop **STEVE JELTZ** of the Philadelphia Phillies pulled the hidden-ball trick on **GARY CARTER** of the New York

Mets, probably the man in the ball park who appreciated it the most was former major league shortstop **GENE MICHAEL**. Michael, a New York Yankee executive, was considered the master of the hidden-ball trick. He had perfected the art but only pulled it off five times. Said Michael: "I could have done it more but I was afraid somebody would beat me up."

GEORGE SCOTT, slick fielding Boston Red Sox first baseman, on hitting: "When you're hitting the ball, it comes up to the plate looking like a grapefruit. When you're not hitting, it looks like a black-eyed pea."

Boston Red Sox star **DWIGHT EVANS** after striking out three times against knuckleballer **CHARLIE HOUGH** of Texas: "I was glad when **PHIL NEIKRO** quit, and now I hope Charlie has enough money so that he'll quit. I think he should spend more time with his family."

Former Milwaukee slugger **GORMAN THOMAS** had some big days at the plate, but he claims that the only time he got a standing ovation was in 1975 when he struck out eight straight times and hit into a double play in a series at Boston: "I got a standing ovation for striking out," he said, "a standing ovation for hitting into a double play, and, when I got out to center field, a dog ran out in front of me and relieved himself, and I got another standing ovation."

DON ZIMMER, the Chicago Cubs manager, after his team went 4–4 on a recent road trip: "It just as easily could have gone the other way."

MILLIE SCHEMBECHLER, on her husband's move from Michigan football coach to president of baseball's Detroit Tigers: "Now Bo can finally buy the players he wants."

With the ever-present thought of baseball's longest strike on his mind, Montreal Expos' general manager **KEVIN MALONE** bemoaned his predicament while stating: "For years we've been constantly on the lookout for a shortstop who can pick it. Now we are looking for one who won't."

EARL WEAVER, quick-witted manager of the Baltimore Orioles, when told by slump-ridden outfielder **AL BUMBREY** that he was about to go to chapel services: "Don't forget to take your bat with you."

TED TURNER, owner of the Atlanta Braves, on at least utilizing his team as a tax shelter: "They're a shelter all right. A bomb shelter."

RON LUCIANO, author and former major league umpire: "Being an umpire is a lot like being a king. It prepares you for nothing."

Former Baltimore Oriole right-hander **JIM PALMER**, who was recently elected to the Baseball Hall of Fame: "I've heard Boston Red Sox pitcher **ROGER CLEMENS** say, 'I'm trying to get into the Hall of Fame.' But I never thought about that. I was trying to get ready for the next game or season; that was consuming enough. Hall of Fame honors are garnered over a long time. It's like pitching in the first inning and thinking about what you are going to do in the ninth."

Slugger **HANK AARON**: "The pitcher has got only a ball. I've got a bat. So the percentage in weaponry is in my favor, and I let the fellow with the ball do the fretting."

Former Cleveland pitching great and Hall of Famer **BOB FELLER**: "Baseball is a kid's game that grown-ups only tend to screw up."

Former California Angels manager **LEFTY PHILLIPS**, explaining his teams' slump: "Our phenoms ain't phenominating."

Pitching star **NOLAN RYAN**: "It helps if the hitters think you're a little crazy."

St. Louis Cardinals trainer **GENE GIESELMANN**, on the rash of injuries during the first weeks of the baseball season: "We have three leagues now; the N.L. (National League), the A.L. (American League), and the D.L. (Disabled League)."

Los Angeles Dodgers' Hall of Fame pitcher **SANDY KOUFAX**: "Pitching is the art of instilling fear."

Former Pittsburgh Pirates slugger **WILLIE STARGELL**: "They give you a round bat and they throw a round ball, and they tell you to hit it square."

Former Brooklyn Dodgers outfielder **CARL FURILLO**: "Carrots might be good for my eyes, but they won't straighten out the curve ball."

Former New York Mets first baseman **KEITH FERNAN-DEZ**, on synthetic baseball fields: "Rugs belong on bald heads. They're bad for baseball."

Former Milwaukee Brewers outfielder **JIM WOHLFORD**: "Ninety percent of this game is half mental."

Pittsburgh Pirates second baseman **JOSE LIND**—a native of Puerto Rico—on winning his arbitration case for $2 million: "America! What a country."

Former major league relief pitcher **KEVIN HICKEY**: "Things were going so badly for me that when I tried to stay at Motel 6, they'd turned off the light."

Former New York Yankee pitcher **JIM BOUTON**, author of *Ball Four*: "You spend a good piece of your life gripping a baseball and, in the end, it turns out that it was the other way around all the time."

Pittsburgh Pirates outfielder **ANDY VAN SLYKE**: "Every season has its peaks and valleys. What you have to try to do is eliminate the Grand Canyon."

Former Baseball Commissioner **A. BARTLETT GIAMATTI**: "(Baseball) is designed to break your heart. The game begins in the spring, when everything else begins again, and it blossoms in the summer, filling the afternoons and evenings, and then as soon as the chill rains come, it stops and leaves you to face the fall alone."

Former pitcher **DON SUTTON** to a reporter who had been interviewing Dodger manager **TOM LASORDA**: "You know what you can do with all those notes you took? Shred 'em and put 'em around the shrubs at home and watch them grow."

National League umpire **BILL KLEM**: "Sure I muffed a few in my time. But I never called one wrong in my heart."

JUAN BENIQUEZ, who played for eight American League baseball teams: "I'll make a career going to old timers' games.

Great Boston Braves and Milwaukee Braves Hall of Fame pitcher **WARREN SPAHN**, asked if he ever iced his arm: "Ice is for mixed drinks."

New York Yankee catcher **YOGI BERRA**: "I never blame myself when I'm not hitting. I just blame the bat, and if it keeps up, I change bats. After all if I know it isn't my fault that I'm not hitting, how can I get mad at myself?"

Former Detroit Tigers pitcher **JACK MORRIS**, when the Tigers led the American League East by four and a half games: "This team has unbelievable pitching. Thank God."

New York Yankees relief pitcher **SPARKY LYLE**: "Why pitch nine innings when you can get just as famous pitching two?"

Former St. Louis Cardinals' great **DIZZY DEAN**: "The good Lord was good to me. He gave me a strong body, a good right arm, and a weak mind."

BILLY RIPKEN, when the Baltimore Orioles unveiled new uniforms including the replacement of a cartoon bird with an ornithologically correct Oriole on the caps: "I hope it flies better than the other one."

BILL VEECK, owner of the Chicago White Sox: "Baseball is almost the only orderly thing in a very unorderly world. If you get three strikes, even the best lawyer in the world can't get you off."

Red Sox pitcher **DENNIS "OIL CAN" BOYD** after **BO JACKSON** hit a mammoth home run against him at Fenway Park: "That was serious contact, man. It went 800 feet. Nobody ever done that to me before."

Baseball's **DON BAYLOR** when asked what he thought of **TOM KELLY**, his manager when he played for the Minnesota Twins: "One of the weirdest people I've ever met in baseball."

Texas Rangers knuckleballer **CHARLIE HOUGH,** after catcher **DON SLAUGHT** committed four passed balls in his six innings of work: "I had a real good knuckle ball tonight. I had no idea where I was throwing it."

Former St. Louis Cardinals catcher **JOE GARAGIOLA,** after going out to dinner with the manager of the Los Angeles Dodgers: "Having dinner with **TOMMY LASORDA** is like pitching a game in the big leagues. Afterwards you need three days rest."

PAT GILLICK, Toronto Blue Jays general manager, on the demand of thirty-nine-year-old outfielder **RICO CARTY** for a long-term contract: "I don't mind paying for a player, but I don't want to pay for his funeral."

RICK BERNALDO, coach of Hillsborough of Tampa, after a thirty-two-inning win over Manatee of Bradenton in a Florida Community College game: "One of our guys slid into second base in the first inning and his scab had healed by the end of the game."

RON SWOBODA, former New York Mets outfielder: "Why am I wasting so much dedication on a mediocre career?"

JIM FREY, former Kansas City Royal manager, asked what advice he gives to George Brett on hitting: "I tell him, 'Attaway to hit, George.'"

Cleveland Indians pitcher **TOM CANDIOTTI**, on discussing knuckle balls with teammate **PHIL NIEKRO**: "It was like talking to **THOMAS EDISON** about light bulbs."

KEN COLEMAN, Boston Red Sox broadcaster, gushing over a long home run by first baseman **BOB WATSON**: "They usually show movies on a flight like that."

DENNIS LAMP, Chicago Cub pitcher, whose pitching hand was badly bruised when **LOU BROCK** caromed a ball off it for his 3,000th hit: "I guess they'll be sending my fingers to Cooperstown."

DON BAYLOR, Colorado Rockies manager, after being ejected by umpire **GREG BONIN** for disputing a strike call, when asked if he had bumped Bonin: "If I did, I didn't bump him hard enough, because he was still standing."

BRITT BURNS, Chicago White Sox pitcher: "I think too much on the mound sometimes, and I get brain cramps."

DAN SHAUGHNESSY, Boston Globe sportswriter: "Defensively the Red Sox are a lot like Stonehenge. They are old, they don't move, and no one is certain why they are positioned the way they are."

MITCH WEBSTER, who had played only with Montreal and Toronto in the major leagues, had this to say when he was traded to the Chicago Cubs: "It'll be great not to have to listen to two national anthems.

New York Mets' announcer **RALPH KINER**, during a game in which the Mets trailed the Philadelphia Phillies 2–1, going into the final inning: "And the Mets need at least one run to tie the score."

YOGI BERRA:
"If you don't know where you are going, you might wind up someplace."
"Always go to other people's funerals, otherwise they won't come to yours."
Reminiscing during a TV interview about New York Yankee battery mate **DON LARSON'S** perfect game in the 1965 World Series: "It's never happened in World Series competition, and it still hasn't."
When asked what he thinks about when standing at home plate with a bat in his hand: "Think? How can you think and hit at the same time?"

The Ryan Express may soon be a road as well as a fast ball. The Texas Senate voted 28–3 to name State Highway 288 that runs past Nolan Ryan's home in Alvin, **THE NOLAN RYAN EXPRESS-WAY**. "This is the only one people drive 92 MPH on," said Senator Buster Brown.

Baltimore Oriole manager **EARL WEAVER**, on former umpire **RON LUCIANO'S** new career as an NBC sportscaster: "I hope he takes this job more seriously than he did his last one."

GENE MAUCH, Minnesota Twins manager, on having a blood relative, **ROY SMALLEY,** on his team: "Sometimes I look on Roy as my nephew, but sometimes only as my sister's son."

GAYLORD PERRY, often suspected of throwing spitballs, was pitching to **AL OLIVER** in the Old-Timers All-Star game in Cincinnati, when Oliver asked the umpire to inspect the ball. That didn't stop Perry. Before the next pitch, he poured a cup of water over the ball. That didn't stop Oliver. He whacked the next pitch for a home run.

Pittsburgh Pirates pitcher **DAVE LAPOINT**, of his days with the San Francisco Giants: "If they keep this team together, we could finish thirty games out of first place."

New York Mets left-hander **FRANK TANANA**, on his evolution as a pitcher: "In the seventies, I threw in the nineties; in the nineties, I throw in the seventies."

Left-handed pitcher **TOMMY JOHN:** "The Yankees are America's team. You know, Mom, apple pie, Gucci loafers, Rolls Royces...."

JOE NIEKRO, Houston Astro twenty-one-game winner in 1979, asked how he expected to pitch this season: "Right-handed."

MIKE MARSHALL, Minnesota relief pitcher, who was booed by fans one season: "If they worked as hard at their jobs as I do at mine, this country wouldn't have the inflation problem it now has."

OSCAR GAMBLE, Texas Ranger outfielder, on his disappointing 1978 season with the San Diego Padres, who had given him a six-year $2.85 million contract: "Most of the San Diego fans didn't even know my name. They just called me 2.85. It was a very long, long year."

Oakland outfielder **JOSE CANSECO** on Dodger pitcher **OREL HERSHISER**: "My first impression is he's a hell of a hitter. I'm going to hire him as my personal hitting coach."

Said Oakland pitcher **DAVE STEWART** to *Newsday* when told Los Angeles Dodger manager **TOM LASORDA** had taken a verbal shot at Stewart's teammate **DON BAYLOR**, after Baylor had taken a shot at the Dodgers: "Just stick some spaghetti in his mouth. That will keep him quiet for a while."

Hall of Fame pitcher **JIM PALMER**, on basketball guard **DANNY AINGE** of the Phoenix Suns, who once played for the Toronto Blue Jays: "No matter how long he played, he could never hit a fastball to the left of the first base coach."

WADE BOGGS of the New York Yankees, on why he did not feel any loyalty to his former team, the Boston Red Sox: "You have pets for loyalty."

St. Louis Cardinals pitcher **JOE MAGRANE,** analyzing a pitching outing: "I had three things working for me tonight—sinker, slider, and bone chips."

San Francisco Giants' announcer **RON FAIRLY** is making a move in the malapropism department. Some of his latest:

"He fakes a bluff."

"Last night I neglected to mention something that bears repeating."

"The Giants are looking for a trade, but I don't think Atlanta wants to depart with a quality player."

When **DON ZIMMER** was manager of the Boston Red Sox, **BILL LEE** was on the pitching staff. Lee termed Zimmer "The Gerbil" and from then on, there was no love lost between the two. A couple of years later, when Zimmer was asked to recall a few Bill Lee stories, he replied: "I'll gladly talk to you about Adolph Hitler, but not Bill Lee."

Sports lawyer **BOB WOOLF**, recalling a contract he once negotiated for **BOB STANLEY** with the Boston Red Sox: "We had statistics showing he was the third-best pitcher in the league. They had a chart showing he was the sixth-best pitcher on the Red Sox."

BERT BLYLEVIN, when pitching for the California Angels, on how he became a pitcher instead of a catcher: "When I started throwing the ball back to the pitcher harder than he was throwing to me, we changed positions."

Former Baltimore Oriole **JOHN LOWENSTEIN** once recommended moving first base back a foot. Why? "To eliminate close plays," he said.

On the day after being knocked out in the fifth inning of a game against Cleveland, Baltimore Oriole pitcher **JIM PALMER** was interviewed on the "Today" show about the revealing ads he appears in for Jockey underwear. "That," noted Baltimore radio personality **LARRY HALL**, "gave Jim two brief appearances in as many days."

SCOTT OSTLER, in the San Francisco *Chronicle*, drawing a comparison between Oakland A's pitchers **GOOSE GOSSAGE**, forty-two, and **TODD VAN POPPEL**, twenty-one: "Gossage's mustache is older than Van Poppel."

Former major league pitcher **JIM "MUDCAT" GRANT**, when asked about the way it was when he pitched in the majors from 1958 through 1971: "Of course we used sandpaper, we used spit, we used stickum, we used grease. We used everything we possibly could."

The Bellevue, Washington, *Journal-American* conducted a slightly different baseball poll, asking the wives of the Seattle Mariners baseball team to vote for the handsomest players in the game. The winner was no surprise: Underwear model **JIM PALMER** of the Baltimore Orioles. He was followed by the Mariners' own **RICK HONEYCUTT**, then **JIM RICE, BUCKY DENT, GEORGE BRETT, JOE SIMPSON** of Seattle, **PAUL MOLITOR, BILL RUSSELL** of the Dodgers, **DWIGHT EVANS** of the Red Sox, and **KEN SINGLETON** of the Orioles. **DEBBIE HONEYCUTT**, wife of the runner-up, said: "The poll was confusing though. We weren't sure if they wanted it from the neck up or from the neck down or both."

Manager **CASEY STENGEL** was fired after the New York Yankees lost the 1960 World Series, and the Yankees tried to soften the announcement by citing his age. Said Stengel: "That settles it. I'll never make the mistake of being seventy again."

JOHN KRUK, the Philadelphia Phillies doughy first baseman, reacting to a prediction by St. Louis Cardinals outfielder **RAY LANKFORD** that the Cards would win the National League East because they're in better shape than the Phils: "He probably looked at our media guide and saw a picture of me."

In a game at Candlestick Park, San Francisco Giant first baseman **WILL CLARK** reached into the stands to catch a foul ball and a fan spilled beer on him. "When I came in when the inning was over, he (the fan) yelled at me, 'You stole my ball,'" Clark said. "I said 'Yeah, and I got your beer too.'"

Former Philadelphia Phillies star **RICHIE ASHBURN** telling his broadcast partner **HARRY KALAS** how he used to take especially good care of his bats, even to the point of sleeping with them: "That's right, Harry. In my day, I went to bed with a lot of old bats."

Remember **ROSS GRIMSLEY**, the left-handed pitcher with the not-so-fast fastball? Sportswriter **DALE STINGER** once said, "Ross Grimsley has three speeds; slow, slower, and hurry up already."

THOMAS BOSWORTH of the *Washington Post* recalled a night in Baltimore when Grimsley's pitches were going out of the ballpark faster then they were coming in to the batters. Finally, manager **EARL WEAVER** went to the mound and told the beleaguered southpaw, "If you know how to cheat, start now."

Was **NOLAN RYAN** always an intimidating pitcher? As a high school senior, he once began a game by splitting the batting helmet of the first hitter and breaking an arm of the second. "The third guy," Ryan remembered, "begged not to hit."

For weeks a Minneapolis man tried to sell his car without success. But when the Minnesota Twins won a spot in the World Series, **BOB DISTAD** got an idea—he offered his four Series tickets to anyone who would buy his car. He put up a sign in his front yard offering his four Series tickets and his four-year-old Chrysler for $8,850. Within hours Distad had sold his tickets and the car.

When the Minnesota Twins signed **DON BAYLOR**, the word was that the club was counting on his experience and leadership to carry them in the stretch drive. Said manager **TOM KELLY**: "I don't believe much in that leadership stuff. We got Don Baylor to hit the ball for us."

From the Sacramento *Bee*: "Remember the tale about Kansas City Royals 'tranquillity coach' **JOHN MAYBERRY**, who got into a shoving match with **BILL BUCKNER?** The 'tranquillity coach' missed the team's next flight because he was in jail. His wife, Janice, filed misdemeanor battery charges against her husband, who was released on a $1,000 recognizance bond."

From former Cleveland Indian reliever **DOUG JONES**, endorsing the drive to build a new ballpark to replace Cleveland Stadium: "Cleveland Stadium is not a baseball park. It's a museum. A museum of unnatural history."

One day after the New York Yankees', nine-game winning streak had ended, Yankees third base coach **GENE MICHAEL** left the club to attend his son's wedding. So **MIKE FERRARO** coached at third. Oakland's third baseman **CARNEY LANSFORD** looked at Ferraro and said, "What's going on here?" Ferraro said, "You know how it goes. You guys won, so somebody had to go."

Cleveland Indians reliever **DOUG JONES**, asked if he goes into another state of mind when he's in a save situation: "I don't know anyone who goes into another mental state, except that guy **OIL CAN BOYD**."

KEITH HERNANDEZ, New York Mets first baseman, on an agonizing pennant race in the National League East: "We've been in the hangman's noose for a week now, only nobody yet has kicked the horse."

YOGI BERRA, New York Yankees catcher, in a discussion of the 1954 season, once said: "**BOBBY AVILA** had a good year for Cleveland. He got the MVP that year, I think. Nineteen fifty-four? I'm pretty sure. Didn't he?" The answer is no. The most valuable player in the American League that year was Yogi Berra.

Chicago Cubs slugger **ANDRE DAWSON**, on the tactical risks taken by manager **DON ZIMMER**: "Suicide squeeze, safety bunt, hit-and-run, just about anything, anytime. I've seen him hit-and-run with the bases loaded, and I've only seen that twice in my entire career."

ELLIS CLARY, Toronto Blue Jays scout, on the size of the Toronto Skydome: "It's big enough for deer hunting."

In a game at St. Louis, San Francisco Giants outfielder **CANDY MALDONADO** had already hit a home run, a triple, and a single when he hit what looked like another triple in the eighth inning. However, according to **JAYSON STARK** of the Philadelphia *Inquirer*, third base coach **DON ZIMMER** held Maldonado up at second base. That gave Maldonado a double, and thus became the first player to hit for the cycle in Busch Stadium since 1975. Said Giant manager **ROGER CRAIG**: "That's why Don Zimmer is regarded as a great third base coach."

Former St. Louis Cardinals catcher **TONY PENA**, fighting his way out of a hitting slump, kept taking extra batting practice until manager **WHITEY HERZOG** told him he was only wearing himself out. Says Herzog: "If batting practice made Hall of Famers, I'd be in it."

Los Angeles Dodgers manager **TOMMY LASORDA** had lost twenty-two pounds since he began his diet, but at some cost. He told **SCOTT NEWMAN** of the Pasadena *Star-News*, "I see giant clams in my sleep."

As he opened a huge container of lasagna before a game at Shea Stadium, **TOMMY LASORDA**, manager of the Los Angeles Dodgers, told a *New York Times* writer: "The mother of the manager of the Hyatt makes this for us whenever we're in New York. Wherever I go, people feed us. I tell my coaches, 'If anybody asked you how you like their food, you tell them, I don't know yet.' That way they keep feeding you."

During trade rumors one winter, former New York Yankee utility player **PHIL LINZ** issued this ultimatum: "Play me or keep me."

TERRY FRANCONA, former baseball major leaguer and now manager of the Birmingham Barons, the White Sox minor league affiliate, on handing out Double A meal money to his famed right fielder: "There's something odd about going up to **MICHAEL JORDAN** and giving him $16 a day."

When asked about the pitching inconsistency of twenty-two-year-old right-hander **SALOMON TORRRES, DICK POLE**, San Francisco Giant pitching coach replied: "It's youth. But that youth thing gets old after a while."

RALPH KINER, former National League batting star and now the New York Mets announcer: "The Mets just had their first .500 or better April since July of 1992."

CLAUDELL WASHINGTON, California Angels outfielder, asked why he went out for track in high school: "Because the track coach was the biology teacher, and I had trouble with biology. I'm not crazy."

MARK McGUIRE, giant first baseman of the Oakland Athletics, on baseball fights: "It doesn't pay to get in the bottom of the pile. You can't do anything, and you're eating grass the whole time."

GEORGE BRETT of the Kansas City Royals, asked if he's bothered by questions about **BO JACKSON**: "When someone comes up to me, they're either going to ask me why I'm batting .230 or about Bo. I'd rather talk about him."

After Cincinnati Reds slugger **ERIC DAVIS** had hit for the cycle, then-manager **PETE ROSE** was asked where he was when **FRANK ROBINSON** hit for the cycle for the Reds in 1959. "I was in high school," Rose told *USA Today*, "and I'm serious. Was that my second year of the tenth grade or my first?"

CHRIS BERMAN, ESPN announcer who pins goofy nicknames on ballplayers, offered: Roberto "Remember the" Alomar,

David "Sili" Cone, Dave "Death" Valle, John "Hia" Wathan, Tom "Cotton" Candiotti, Chili "Con Carne" Davis, and Todd "Mercedes" Benzinger.

Former Pittsburgh Pirates catcher **JUNIOR ORTEZ** told the *Pittsburgh Press* that he's a better catcher at Los Angeles Dodger Stadium because of the ground level box seats behind home plate. "You don't want to have a passed ball there," said Ortez, "because when you run back to the screen you are looking people right in the eye and they're saying, 'Ortez, you are the worst.'"

Every wonder who came up with the idea of draggin' the infield after the fifth inning? Well, it began in the Pacific Coast League in 1949, when manager **FRED HANEY** of the Hollywood Stars decided fans would buy more concessions if there was a ten-minute break in the middle of the game. Haney came up with the brainstorm while pondering a suggestion from concessions chief **DANNY GOODMAN** on how to boost business.

From **MITCH WILLIAMS**, fine major league relief pitcher, contrasting his style to that of starting pitcher **RICK SUTCLIFFE** when they were both with the Chicago Cubs: "I'm out there throwing like my hair's on fire, and he's out there like he's sitting in a lawn chair."

One day in Pittsburgh, writes baseball writer **BILL HONIG**, New York Giants superstar outfielder **WILLIE MAYS** was unable to reach across with his glove to snag a hooking line drive. So he reached out and caught the ball with his barehand. Racing into the dugout after the inning, Mays was expecting a fuss over his unprecedented play. But manager **LEO DUROCHER** has ordered the bench to remain silent. Finally Mays said to Durocher: "Leo, didn't you see what I did out there?" "No," Durocher retorted, "and you're going to have to do it again before I believe it."

Detroit manager **SPARKY ANDERSON**, talking about a player's injured shoulder: "There's nothing wrong with his shoulder except some pain—and pain don't hurt you."

The Yankees had just signed pitcher **RON GUIDRY** to a one-year contract. Was it hard to get new manager **DALLAS GREEN** to agree? "Not at all," **GEORGE STEINBRENNER** said. "I just told him to sign."

ROCKY BRIDGES, former major league infielder: "I got a big charge out of seeing **TED WILLIAMS** hit. Once in a while they let me try to field some of them, which sort of dimmed my enthusiasm."

Hall of Fame pitcher **BOB FELLER**, quoted by the Cleveland *Plain Dealer* on all-time strikeout king **NOLAN RYAN** of the Texas Rangers: "There was only one pitcher faster than I was. That was Walter Johnson. My curve was much better than Ryan's. His is only average."

Former St. Louis Cardinals manager **WHITEY HERZOG**, on his .258 batting average as a center fielder for the Washington Senators: "I was playing between **ROY SIEVERS** and **JIM LEMON**. By the time it was my turn to bat, I was too tired to hit."

ERIC GREGG, 300-pound National League umpire, to a trainer who put him on a rigorous weight-loss program: "Let's not overdo this. I only have to call the bases, not steal them."

California Angels pitcher **JIM ABBOTT**, asked if the wooden bat might eventually be replaced by the livelier aluminum bat in the major leagues: "I'll quit if they go to aluminum bats."

VIDA BLUE, former Oakland Athletics and San Francisco Giants pitcher, was married at the end of a season at Candlestick Park. The ceremony included an honor guard of Giants with raised bats and a carriage ride around the outfield for the newlyweds. When a TV crew approached the groom and asked for an interview, Blue declined because he "didn't want to turn his wedding into a circus."

BOB STANLEY, Boston Red Sox pitcher, noting that Texas Rangers catcher **MIKE STANLEY** had thrown out only two of fifty-one bad runners attempting to steal; "It must be the name. His arm must be as bad as mine. But I'm having a better year. I'm three out of eleven."

Former St. Louis Cardinals manager **WHITEY HERZOG**: "Baseball has been very good to me since I quit trying to play it."

BEN HENKEY of *The Sporting News*, in an obit on former New York Giant first baseman **BILL TERRY**, the last National League player to hit .400, revised this ditty by poet-humorist **OGDEN NASH**:

"T is for Terry
The Giant from Memphis
Whose .400 average
You can't overemphis."

National League slugger **KEVIN MITCHELL**, asked the secret of his success: "I just keep swinging away. Only the mailman walks."

JIM DeSHAIES, Minnesota Twins pitcher, who ignored baseball lore and traditions by changing his seat in the dugout during his teammate **SCOTT ERIKSON'S** recent no-hit pitching masterpiece: "I think everybody gets caught up in all these superstitions. But I don't put much stock in them—knock on wood."

Years ago, when home run production was higher than ever, **RICHARD JUSTICE** of the Washington *Post* asked around the major leagues if the ball was juiced up. Some answers: Detroit outfielder **PAT SHERIDAN**, after hitting the Tiger Stadium light tower in batting practice, said: "I think the balls are made by Titleist now." Kansas City manager **BILLY GARDNER**, bouncing a baseball on the ground, said, "See that? If there was a carrot near it, the ball would eat it." Milwaukee pitching coach **CHUCK HARTENSTEIN** said, "We won't have to buy baseballs this year. We'll just put 'em in the ball bag and let 'em multiply."

Pitcher **CURT SCHILLING** of the Philadelphia Phillies, who had a 16–7 record in 1993, has a simple explanation for his 0–7 start in 1994: "I'm doing all of the little things you need to do to lose games."

DICK "DR. STRANGEGLOVE" STUART, the stone-fingered first baseman and slugger, who joined the Pittsburgh Pirates midway through the 1958 season, helped make them a pennant contender, only to be voted a meager half-share of the bonus money by his teammates, the same amount received by the bat boy. Asked about this seeming slight, Stuart said: "You must understand, he's a very good bat boy."

Famed sportswriter **JIMMY BRESLIN**, in a story about the futile 1962 New York Meets, wrote of the frustrations manager **CASEY STENGEL** encountered with his pitching staff. In a game with the St. Louis Cardinals, Mets pitcher **RAY DAVIAULT** threw a low fastball to the Cardinals batter **CHARLEY JONES**. He hit the pitch deep into the left field stands for the game-winning run. "It was bad luck," Daviault told Stengel. "I threw him a perfect pitch." Casey replied: "It couldn't have been a perfect pitch. Perfect pitches don't travel that far."

From outfielder **TOM BRUNANSKY**, then with the Minnesota Twins: "Ninety-nine percent of the guys in the league with no-trade contracts had it in their contracts they wouldn't play for us. The other one percent were already here."

Philadelphia Phillies third baseman **DAVE HOLLINS** has had great success hitting against Montreal's **BUTCH HENRY**, going twelve for fifteen with five home runs. Said Butch Henry: "I could make him millions."

New York Yankee general manager **GENE MICHAEL**, presenting the National League Cy Young Award to **GREG MADDUX** at the New York baseball dinner after Maddux signed with the Atlanta Braves for $6 million less than the Yankees offered: "I promised to bring Greg Maddux to New York and here he is."

Some baseball teams make it mandatory that a veteran pitcher take a rookie bullpen-mate under his wing. Said **ROGER McDOWELL**, veteran Los Angeles Dodger pitcher, after rookie pitcher **DARREN DREIFORT** was assigned to him: "I have to go to all the places he can't, to make sure he isn't there."

YOGI BERRA, New York Yankee catcher: "Listen up because I've got nothing to say and I'm only going to say it once."

When the Detroit Tigers **BILL MADLOCK** got his 2,000th career hit at Fenway Park, he got a standing ovation from the Boston fans; "I couldn't believe it," he said. "I looked around at the scoreboard to see if a Celtics score had been posted."

MARTY SPRINGSTEAD, who became supervisor of American League umpires, said he would never forget his first assignment behind the plate. It was in a 1965 game at Washington, **FRANK HOWARD** was playing for the Senators, and on the first pitch to the huge slugger, Springstead called a knee-high fastball a strike. Springstead: "Howard turned around and hollered, 'Get something straight, Buster. I don't know where you came from or how you got to the major leagues, but don't call a strike on me with that pitch. Understand?'" The next pitch was in the same spot and Springstead yelled, "Two!" "Two what?" roared Howard. "Too low," said Springstead. "Much too low."

Cincinnati Reds manager **PETE ROSE**, explaining why he wouldn't talk about what he told his players at a team meeting: "That's why we call it a closed-door meeting. If I wanted you to know, I'd have invited you inside."

STEVE FARR, Kansas City Royal relief pitcher, to the suggestion that his shoulder problem might be more mental than physical: "How can it be mental? I don't even have a college education."

Said Boston Red Sox pitcher **DENNIS "OIL CAN" BOYD**, after Red Sox rookie **SAM HORN** launched a tape measure home run shot at Toronto: "I thought they were going to have to check it through customs. I thought he hit it back to the States."

RALPH KINER, National League slugger, while a New York Mets radio announcer, tells a story about **YOGI BERRA'S** attempts to reach his wife, Carmen, by phone when his team was on the road. He spent four hours dialing their home in northern New Jersey without getting an answer. Finally he succeeded in reaching her. "Where have you been?" he demanded. "I went to see 'Dr. Zhivago,'" she said. "What's wrong with you now?" he snapped.

Former Brewer outfielder **GORMAN THOMAS** on Milwaukee fans: "They know when to cheer, and they know when to boo, and they know when to drink beer—and that's all the time."

Said former major leaguer **RALPH RAMIREX** when asked why so few players from the Dominican Republic get walked: "You have to swing like a man. A walk won't get you off the island."

KEITH MORELAND of the Chicago Cubs on teammate **ANDRE DAWSON**: "I expect the phone to ring anytime and someone at the other end to say, 'You can't have Andre anymore. He's been called up to a higher league.'"

WHITEY HERZOG, St. Louis Cardinals manager and a man of few words, on why pitchers are getting so many more strikeouts: "Because more hitters are striking out."

During a Phillies-Braves National League Conference playoff showdown, Philadelphia reliever **LARRY ANDERSON** confided in Atlanta's **TERRY PENDELTON**: "If we don't win this series, I hope you guys do."

Said former Pittsburgh Pirates pitcher **BRIAN FISHER** after getting his first major league hit, a home run against Cincinnati: "I got a little lucky. The ball hit the bat and jumped out of the ballpark. When it went over the fence, I said to myself, 'What do I do now?'"

DAVE COLLINS of the Cincinnati Reds, agreeing with many other major leaguers that the baseballs are "juiced up": "My ten-hop singles are getting through the infield on eight hops."

Hall of Famer **WILLIE STARGELL**, who hit an opponent record fifty-nine runs at New York Mets' Shea Stadium, on a comment that Shea is a difficult park in which to hit homers: "Difficult for whom?"

Said Philadelphia Phillies third baseman **MIKE SCHMIDT**, when asked what he will miss most in baseball when he retired: "Room service and French fries."

R.J. REYNOLDS of the Pittsburgh Pirates on the low attendance at Three Rivers Stadium: "Sometimes you walk out onto the field and you wonder if they've opened the gates."

When Hall of Famer **FRANKIE FRISCH** was managing the Chicago Cubs, he watched pitcher **BOB MUNCRIEF** give up a home run to the Pittsburgh Pirates slugger **RALPH KINER** on a curveball. Frisch went to the mound and told Muncrief: "Never give Kiner a curve. Throw him nothing but fastballs." Next time up, Kiner got hold of a fastball and hit it about nine miles. As Frisch came to the mound, Muncrief said: "Well, Frank, he hit your pitch a lot farther than he hit mine."

Former Chicago Cub announcer **STEVE STONE** on Los Angeles Dodger manager **TOMMY LASORDA**, who is known for his hefty eating habits: "His license plate says, 'Honk if you have groceries.'"

The subject was hitting, or lack of it, and the conversation got around to **HANK AGUIRRE**, a former major league pitcher who was a notoriously bad hitter. **FRANK LUKSA** of the Dallas *Times* recalled a game in which Aguirre, a career .085 hitter, managed to hit a triple. In a fit of optimism, he then threatened to steal home. Said the third base coach: "Hank, it took you thirteen years to get here, so don't fool around."

The Philadelphia Phillies were mired in a losing streak, and the city was in the grips of a heat wave. Before one game, there was considerable griping among players about the weather, when manager **GENE MAUCH** suddenly exploded. "That's enough!" he shouted. "I don't want to hear anymore. The first guy I hear complaining about the heat during the game is going to pay for it." After the first inning, Phillies' outfielder **JOHNNY CALLISON**, his uniform soaked with sweat, staggered into the dugout. "God, it's hot," he said, stopping suddenly as he spotted Mauch out of the corner of his eye. "Just the way I like it."

When **PETE ROSE** was in the major leagues, he didn't chew tobacco, not that he didn't give it a try. He tells about his first experience with the stuff when he broke in with Cincinnati under manager **FRED HUTCHINSON**. "I didn't like the taste of it and I told Hutch," Rose said. "Hutch told me to mix the chew with gum. After giving his suggestions a try for a week, I told him I still wasn't feeling well, and Hutch asked me what I did about the juices. I said, 'What juices?'"

New York Mets' announcer **RALPH KINER**, continuing his bid for the malapropos Hall of Fame, came up with this one on a June 21 date: "On this Father's Day, we again wish you all a happy birthday."

When a pitcher gets into trouble, does he appreciate it when a teammate comes to the mound to counsel him? Not always. Said former catcher **TIM McCARVER**, recalling his days with the St. Louis Cardinals: "I remember one time going out to the mound to talk to right hand pitching star **BOB GIBSON**. He told me to get back behind the batter, that the only thing I knew about pitching was that it was hard to hit."

Former Cleveland third baseman **AL ROSEN** will never forget a visit he made to pitcher **ART HOUTTEMAN**. Houtteman told him, "If you know so much about pitching, then you do it." With that Houtteman flipped the ball to Rosen and walked off the mound.

Then there was the great **LEFTY GROVE** who, after a teammate came over to remind him the bases were loaded, fixed the informant with an icy stare and sneered, "I didn't think they gave me three extra fielders."

Boston Red Sox right-hander **DANNY DARWIN**, who suffered from an inflamed sciatica tendon in spring training: "I knew I was psychotic, but I didn't know I was sciatic."

After the Florida Marlins stranded seventeen runners in a game against Philadelphia, Phillies first baseman **JOHN KRUK** said, "It was Meet the Marlins Night."

JERRY COLEMAN, San Diego Padres announcer: "The squeeze bunt works less often than it succeeds."

Baseball's effort to speed up games, reduced the average length of a game by five minutes. Wrote **STEVEN ROSENBLOOM** of the Chicago *Sun-Times*: "It's like cutting two pages from *War and Peace*.

It was vintage **BILL LEE**, Montreal Expos pitcher, following a pep talk to the pennant contending club by its president **JOHN McHALE**. Deadpanned Lee: "He said we'd come a long way but we'd only come from St. Louis." Lee was on the disabled list and had a 3–6 record, and a 5.51 ERA, when he uttered those words. This prompted Expo manager **DICK WILLIAMS** to answer: "Lee sounds a lot funnier when he's winning."

Florida Marlins scouting director **GARY HUGHES**, after watching a 450-foot home run by Double A catcher **CHARLES JOHNSON**: "It was way, way out. If this were the 1960s, I'd say it was far out."

When Major League umpire **ERIC GREGG** checked into a Philadelphia weight-reduction center in the off-season, they couldn't weigh him because the scale only goes to 350 pounds. So they took him down to the Post Office where they put him on the freight scale. He registered 358 pounds. Confessing that he eats too much, he told **STAN HOCHMAN** of the Philadelphia *Daily News*: "The problem is that hotels today have twenty-four hour room service, and that's really killing me."

Detroit Tigers pitcher **WALT TERRELL**, after getting knocked out of the box early in a game against the New York Yankees: "I was so wild I would have walked Manute Bol (7'–7") four times."

TV sportscaster **DICK ENBERG**, recalling his days as a Little League umpire: "When parents and kids started arguing with me as I walked to my car after the game ended, I knew $7.50 per game wasn't enough."

The San Jose *Mercury News* reported this exchange between San Francisco Giants announcers **RON FAIRLY** and **DUANE KULPER** in an item headed, "Would You Repeat That Please?"

Kulper: "It doesn't hurt as much as when you get beat as it does when you beat yourself."

Fairly: "I know just what you're saying. In other words, what you're saying is that you can get beat, and then on the other hand you can beat yourself."

Joe Gergen of *Newsday* points out that **JACK CLARK** had more going for him than **REGGIE JACKSON** did when he became a Yankee. "It wasn't until Jackson earned the designation of Mr. October with a Yankee Stadium performance worthy of a legend that a candy bar bearing his name was placed on the market. The Clark Bar has been available for decades," wrote Gergen.

Jayson Stark of the Philadelphia *Inquirer* says that one of the big questions in New York was whether then-Mets' radio announcer and former National League star **RALPH KINER** can keep up the awesome malapropos pace he has set for himself. The latest Kinerism: "The Mets had gotten their leadoff batter on base only once in this inning." Another. Explaining that the Mets would be playing a twilight game in Los Angeles, he said; "The game will start at 5 P.M. Pacific Coast League daylight time."

Bob Hertzel of the *Pittsburgh Press* said that Pirate catcher **JUNIOR ORTIZ** was having so much trouble catching balls early in the season that he was sent to an eye specialist. The specialist couldn't find anything wrong with Ortiz's eyes, but his contact lenses were another story. "He hadn't cleaned them in six months," said Pirate general manager **SYD THRIFT**, "he couldn't see a thing."

Baseball players are usually aware that their occupation doesn't involve a great deal of security. **GENE MICHAEL**, after taking over as manager of the Chicago Cubs midway through the season: "Right now, **DAVEY LOPES** is our best player. He hits for power, steals bases, gets on base, and plays three or four different positions." The next week, Lopes was traded to Houston.

Said Boston Red Sox infielder **GLENN HOFFMAN** after being recalled from Pawtucket, Rhode Island, home of the Red Sox's affiliate in the International League: "Pawtucket was a lot bigger city on the way up than on the way down." That recalls a quote by much-traveled pitcher **MICKEY MAHLER** of the Texas Rangers: "Every player who has played three straight years in the major leagues should be sent back to the Triple-A league for a month, just to let them see what it is like so they won't forget how good they have it." The next day, the Rangers sent Mahler to their Triple-A team in Oklahoma City.

Here is what **BILL JAMES** had to say about **PHIL GARNER** of the Los Angeles Dodgers in his "Baseball Abstract" of 1986 as he was rated ninth among National League third basemen: "What can you say! Phil Garner is still Phil Garner. He's always been Phil Garner, and he'll always be Phil Garner."

CHUCK TANNER, when he was manager of the Atlanta Braves: "I'm fortunate and blessed. Everyday I put on a uniform I feel like I'm thirteen years old."

San Francisco Giants slugger **KEVIN MITCHELL**, who claims he never lost a fight as a teenage gang member in San Diego, told the *Sporting News*: "I didn't think much of jocks. I used to date (All-American football player) Marcus Allen's sister when he was a big high school star, but I didn't like him. He was a bully. But we're friends now."

RON KITTLE of the New York Yankees, after pitcher **BILL LONG** of the Chicago White Sox beat the Yankees 2–0 on a two-hitter: "It was a **Long** night."

Several years ago, shortstop **FREDDIE PATEK** hit three home runs and a double, leading the California Angels to a 20–2 rout of the Boston Red Sox. Patek stood 5'–5" and weighed 148 pounds. Of his short stature, he said: "I'd rather be the shortest player in the major leagues than the tallest in the minors."

From the Boston *Globe*: "Iberian Peninsula Matchup: Before the year is out, with any luck, we might get to see Minnesota pitcher **MARK PORTUGAL** pitch against Milwaukee's **ALEX MADRID**. Meanwhile we're still waiting for Minnesota's **ALLAN ANDERSON** to pitch against Cleveland's **ANDY ALLANSON**."

Houston Astros **PHIL GARNER** on his days with the Pittsburgh Pirates when the club had nine different uniform combinations: "We never knew what we were going to look like. One day we'd look like bumblebees. The next day, you couldn't see us. Then we'd look like a bunch of taxicabs running around the field."

NEAL HEATON, a twenty-seven-year-old left-hander for the Montreal Expos, who pitched five years in the American League, had never batted in college, the minor leagues, or the major leagues before this season. Midway in the season, he was eleven for thirty-four, a .324 average.

RON DAVIS, former Minnesota Twins' relief pitcher, has a rather interesting interpretation of the word "charisma." Said Davis, who was the recipient of a chorus of boos from the Twins fans for giving up late-game home runs in his late game relief appearances: "When it's ten years later and they still hate you, that's what you call charisma."

When the Pittsburgh Pirates were in Los Angeles to play the Dodgers, Pirates' player **JIM MORRISON** got a ticket for jaywalking. Said the *Sporting News*: "Morrison noted that the public officer estimated his speed at one MPH."

After a fan in Cincinnati complained through the media about all the spitting the players were doing on the field and in the dugout, the Reds were asked for their reaction. Said publicist **JOHN BRAUDE**, after making a statement in defense of the players: "You probably expected me to say that."

Chicago Cubs announcer **STEVE STONE**, giving high marks to all the announcers who have been filling in for veteran announcer **HARRY CARAY**, said that nobody yet had topped actor **BILL MURRAY**, who had blatantly insulted the rest of the league during his anniversary stint. One of Murray's lines: "I hate the New York Mets more than the communists. At least the communists don't have off-season problems."

When the San Francisco Giants lost to the St. Louis Cardinals in the National League playoffs, the players weren't the only ones who were upset. Some women took it badly. Since the Giants were beaten, it had been more difficult to find proper male companionship at restaurants and night clubs. **JACQUELINE LAKOCY** said that she knew very little about baseball but she had hoped to go out and meet lots of men. Said Lakocy, a twenty-six-year-old financial consultant: "It's really sad. If the Giants had won, we would have met happier men."

Oakland Athletics pitcher **STORM DAVIS**, on people calling him lucky to be 19–7 this year: "Every time I do an interview, it's like I'm giving a deposition."

31

A lot of people thought it was a gimmick when Cleveland Indians owner **BILL VEECK** signed forty-two-year-old **SATCHEL PAIGE** during the 1948 season but player-manager **LOU BOUDREAU** found out differently, and it didn't take long. "It was eight o'clock in the morning at the Municipal Stadium," Boudreau told Bill Parillo of the Providence *Journal.* "I met Satch and told him, 'Okay, you can do a little running to get loose.' He just shook his head and said, 'No need to run, Mr. Lou—he always called me Mr. Lou— 'I'm ready now.' "I stepped into the batting cage," said Boudreau, who batted .355 that season, and Satch must have thrown maybe fifteen to twenty pitches to me. I think I was able to hit one or two of those pitches out of the batting cage. Right then I knew he could help us." Paige went 6–1 with a 2.48 ERA (Earned Run Average), and Cleveland won the American League pennant.

San Francisco Giants star pitcher **JOHN BURKETT** was being hit unusually hard in a game with the Colorado Rockies. In the usual post-game interview, Burkett, upon being asked which one of his pitches gave him the most trouble, answered; "The one that was coming out of my hand."

Baseball seasons end but the quotes linger on. The following are from a list compiled by Dave Van Dyck and Joe Goddard of the Chicago *Sun-Times*:

—San Francisco's **ROGER MASON**, on giving up three straight homers to San Diego hitters to start the game: "I'm glad I didn't have a fourth pitch."

—St. Louis Cardinals manager **WHITEY HERZOG**, on the early problems of start relief pitcher **TODD WORRELL**: "His location of pitches is bad—in the seats."

—Minnesota Twins right-handed pitcher **BERT BLYLEVEN**, on leading the major leagues in home runs allowed: "It's pretty bad when your family asks for passes to the game and wants to sit in the left field bleachers."

—**BOB BOONE**, California Angels catcher, on breaking **AL LOPEZ**'s record for number of games caught: "It means I've taken more aspirin than any other player in history."

—Toronto's **RICK LEACH**, on a game the Blue Jays lost to the New York Yankees, 15–14: "Maybe this means we will get an arena football team."

TED WILLIAMS, after hitting .254 for the Boston Red Sox in 1959 at the age of forty-one, was sent the same contract for 1960 by Red Sox owner **TOM YAWKEY**. The contract, calling for $125,000, was the highest salary in baseball. According to legend, Williams sent the contract back. Not for a raise. He wanted a cut in the amount. Williams told Yawkey he would not return to play another season unless Yawkey cut his pay the full amount allowable in those days, 25 percent. Williams forced the owner to pay him $31,250 less because he was embarrassed to hit in the .250s. He played one more year, hit .316, and then retired, without ever asking for his money back. The above can safely be categorized in the "It Wouldn't Happen Now" department.

Except for Brett Saberhagen, it had been tough going for the Kansas City Royals starting pitchers, but relief pitcher **DAN QUISENBERRY** promised it wouldn't last. "It just can't continue," he told the *Sporting News*. "All the top guys, the Steve Carltons, the Don Suttons, had rough times. Tommy John has been half dead before. The good ones always bounce back. As to how they did it, you have to buy their novels."

Who was the most overpaid player in the major leagues in 1989? Richard Justice of the Washing *Post* notes that the San Francisco Giants signed journeyman relief pitcher **KARL BEST** to a $105,000 contract just before spring training. "Best threw only two rounds of batting practice before undergoing elbow surgery and spent the entire year on the disabled list. Thus he'll be paid a full playoff share—about $105,000. "Not all of the Giants are happy about that." Player representative Brett Butler said, "Half the guys on the team don't even know who he is."

Texas Rangers manager **BOBBY VALENTINE** on Detroit Tigers manager **SPARKY ANDERSEN**: "Sparky is so full of it, it's unbelievable. Mark McGuire hits something like six home runs against the Tigers, and when the Tigers are all done with Oakland, he's saying that McGuire is one of the great high-ball hitters. Everybody knows McGuire is a low-ball hitter, but Sparky's hoping some of the managers in his division will start throwing low-ball to McGuire. Unbelievable!"

Said Pittsburgh Pirates pitcher **NEIL HEATON** when asked by Bob Hertzel of the Pittsburgh *Press* what he would do if he made baseball commissioner for a day: "I'd make it a rule that every mound in the National League had to be like the mound at (Los Angeles) Dodger Stadium," wrote Hertzel. "Rules say the mound must be ten inches high. The mound at Dodger Stadium, some players in the league say, is at least double that. They should call it Mount Lasorda."

From outfielder **LLOYD MOSEBY**, who expected to be traded by the Toronto Blue Jays: "For nine years, I've played in pajamas in the worst ballpark in baseball. Now they're going to get real uniforms and play in a real stadium, and I'm not going to get a chance to be part of it."

When someone complained about **PETE INCAVIGLIA'S** numerous strikeouts, Texas Rangers manager **BOBBY VALENTINE** said: "The road to the Hall of Fame is paved with guys who led their leagues in strikeouts." Gerry Fraley of the Atlanta *Journal and Constitution* looked it up and found that Valentine was right. Babe Ruth, Jimmy Foxx, Hank Greenberg, Mickey Mantle, Harmon Killebrew, Hack Wilson, Ralph Kiner, Duke Snider, and Eddie Matthew all were league leaders in strikeouts.

The way Steve Jacobson of *Newsday* figures, New York Yankee manager **LOU PINELLA** should worry about Sundays. Historically that's the day that Yankee owner George Steinbrenner likes to drop the ax. "The owner likes to make a media crash on a Sunday when he can trump the competition," Jacobson said. "He fired Gene Michael the first time on the Sunday the pro football season opened and fired Bob Lemon on the second time on a Sunday. He fired Yogi Berra on a Sunday and chose the Sunday of the fifth game of a World Series to name Pinella manager."

ERNIE BANKS, all star shortstop of the Chicago Cubs and Hall of Famer, is highly optimistic about the longevity of major league baseball despite its strike problems. "You just have to be patient," he says. "Spending thirty years with the Cubs, I learned to be patient."

The Soviet Union National baseball team played its first game and lost 22–0 to a Nicaraguan team, the TASS Agency reported. The visitors led 10–0 after the second inning of the game, played in the Ukrainian capital of Kiev. TASS reported that the Soviets "at least managed to prevent the guests from scoring points in two innings."

LENNY DYKSTRA, Philadelphia Phillies All-Star outfielder, on the baseball strike: "I didn't think we'd get to play this early. I thought it would be like hockey. And it would have been except for some woman (Federal Judge Sonia Sotomayor) who probably had never seen a baseball game, who wouldn't know if Barry Bonds was a car salesman or the best player in the game."

From New York Giants outfielder **BILLY NORTH**: "Young horses run fast; old horses know the way."

From former baseball star **PETE ROSE**, making like **NORM CROSBY**: "All I want is for my case to be heard in front of an impractical decision-maker."

Were the **DEAN** brothers as zany as their nicknames, **DIZZY** and **DAFFY**? Some say they weren't, but famed sportswriter **GRANTLAND RICE** told of a time Daffy was swigging on a soda pop as a train carrying the St. Louis Cardinals entered a tunnel. Rice overheard this exchange: Daffy: "Diz, you tried any of this stuff?" Dizzy: "Just fixin' to. Why?" Daffy: "Don't, I did and I've gone plumb blind."

JOE TORRE, St. Louis Cardinals manager, talked with the Cardinals' fine hitting prospect **DIMITRA YOUNG** about his diet. Torre asked Young, who has a **KEVIN MITCHELL** body, what he normally eats for breakfast. "Lunch," replied the young slugger. A few weeks later, Torre again asked Young about his diet. Young said he was eating lots of salad. So Torre asked him what kind of salad dressing he used. "House," answered Young.

JOE OLIVER, Cincinnati Red catcher, on being surprised that he had to dial a call while visiting a teammate in Montreal's Queen Elizabeth Hospital: "I didn't think they still had rotator phones."

REGGIE JACKSON, Hall of Fame outfielder, on why he dislikes interviews: "Because you have to lie so much."

Cincinnati Reds outfielder **RON GANT** says at first he was bothered by the gyrations of Montreal Expos rookie pitcher **CARLOS PEREZ**, who reacts wildly after each strikeout of an opposing batter. "I thought he was trying to show people up," Gant said, "but now that I've met him I realize he's just goofy."

JOHN LOWENSTEIN, Baltimore Orioles utility outfielder, on how he stays ready to play when called upon: "I flush the john between innings to keep my wrists strong."

BILLY MARTIN, after being named manager of the Oakland Athletics, on his success at teaching fundamentals to his new team: "I taught in New York but not too many of the players listened. The players here in Oakland have bigger ears."

RICHIE HEBNER, Detroit Tiger third baseman and a grave digger during the off-season, after finishing a two-mile run ordered by manager **SPARKY ANDERSON**: "I've buried people in better shape than I'm in."

JOHN McHALE, Montreal Expo general manger, speaking of player agents: "They love it when you're out when they call you. Then when you call them back they can negotiate as long as they want to, at your expense."

GEORGE STEINBRENNER, New York Yankee owner, responding to commissioner **BOWIE KUHN**'s latest lament against free agency because the Yankees had signed pitchers **TOMMY JOHN** and **LUIS TIANT**: "I don't agree with free agency, but it wasn't my leadership that created it."

DICK ERICKSON, head groundskeeper at Metropolitan Stadium in Bloomington, Minnesota, asked what his job would be when the Twins and Vikings move into the domed stadium in 1981: "I guess I'll just scrape the bubble gum off the field."

SPARKY ANDERSON, after his appointment as the new manager of the Detroit Tigers: "It's a terrible thing to have to tell your fans, who have waited like Detroit's have, that their team won't win the pennant this year. But it's better then lying to them."

MICKEY RIVERS, Texas Ranger outfielder, on hearing ex-New York Yankee teammate **REGGIE JACKSON** brag about having an IQ of 160: "Out of what? A thousand?"

EDWARD BENNET WILLIAMS, new owner of the Baltimore Orioles, on why he had been inactive in the free-agent market: "Loyalty, friendship, health, love, and an American League pennant."

PAT PAOLELLA, catcher on the American University baseball team, describing his ambition in life: "My idea of paradise is to be the bullpen coach for the Toledo Mud Hens, live in a trailer, and go fishing with a big chaw of tobacco and ripplesole shoes."

ROCKY BRIDGES, manager of the Pacific Coast League's Phoenix Giants, on his rural Idaho home: "I live so far out in the sticks that when I want to go hunting, I walk toward town."

WILLIE STARGELL, great Pittsburgh Pirates slugger, explaining why he never became one of baseball's free agents: "You pull up an old tree from the ground and move it, say, to California, well, you can damage the roots."

Several years ago, "**BARRY BONDS** made a salary eleven times what Gen. Schwarzkopt did," pointed out **DAN MOFFET** of the Palm Beach (Florida) *Post*. "He wanted to make forty-three times what Gen. Schwarzkopt makes, but the Pittsburgh Pirates took him to arbitration and now he has to settle for only thirty-one times what Gen. Schwarzkopt makes or $2.3 million."

Boston *Globe* columnist **BOB RYAN** says, "What baseball star **BARRY BONDS** needs is a good spanking. I've always said the trouble with baseball is too many Californians (Bonds is from Riverside, California) and too many Spock babies. I also felt that there were too few people willing to tell these spoiled narcissists exactly where to go. This is why (Pirate manager) **JIM LELAND** is my new hero."

One rather warm day at the New York Yankees spring training camp in St. Petersburg, Florida, a distinguished white haired lady approached Yankees catcher Yogi Berra. "Good morning Mr. Berra," she said, "you look mighty cool today." Yogi replied, "Thank you, ma'am. You don't look so hot yourself."

PART 2

BASKETBALL

A Brief History

Basketball, the most widely played and one of the world's most popular team sports, requires of individual players a unique blend of athletic skills on both offense and defense. Today virtually all American elementary schools, high schools, and colleges have basketball programs or teams. Although not intended to be a "contact" sport, basketball nevertheless involves a good deal of physical interaction.

James Naismith was a physical education instructor at the International Young Men's Christian Association Training School (now Springfield College) in Springfield, Massachusetts. In 1891, his chairman assigned Naismith the task of organizing some type of game to fill the months between fall football and spring baseball. The only restriction was that the game had to be played indoors, for the students balked at the idea of outdoor activities in the New England winter.

Naismith at first attempted to adapt outdoor games such as soccer, lacrosse, and rugby to indoor play. This did not work out well. The sports were unsuitable for a confined area and resulted in broken windows and injured players. Finally he settled on the idea of a non-contact sport in which players were not allowed to run with the ball. He arranged for a janitor to hang a peach basket on the balcony at each end of the gymnasium. Dividing his eighteen students into two teams, he gave them a soccer ball to play with and posted his original "thirteen rules" on the bulletin board. One of the main rules made running with the ball a violation. The purpose of the new game was to have players shoot the ball into the basket and prevent the other team from doing the same. The first game was played in December 1891. Only one basket was scored, and the janitor had to climb a ladder to retrieve the ball!

Some observers suggested that the newly invented game be called "Naismith ball" but its originator gave it the name "basketball" instead.

American basketball courts are slightly larger than international courts and measure fifty feet wide by ninety-four feet long. A successful shot, or field goal, is worth two points, or when taken beyond a specified distance (marked by a line) from the basket, three points. A successful foul shot is worth one point.

Sports Quotes and Anecdotes

BASKETBALL

Basketball coach **JIM VALVANO** describing how cheap Villanova coach **ROLLIE MASSIMINO** was on a trip to Italy: "He kept saying what a great hotel we were in, then on the last day he complained the towels were so thick, he couldn't close his suitcase."

CHARLIE ECKMAN relating how he learned he was fired as the coach of the Detroit Pistons: "The club owner told me they were making a change in my department and I said okay. Then I realized I was the only person in my department."

DAVID GLASSMAN, about the book, *Playing for Knight*, by former Indiana player **STEVE ALFORD**: "Alford provides all the depth and insight into Knight's complex character you would expect from a twenty-three-year-old. None."

CHUCK DALY, Detroit Pistons coach and noted clothes horse, after seeing a $1,300 virgin wool suit in a New York store: "I'd rather have something for around $300 from a sheep that fooled around a little."

HUBIE BROWN, one of the National Basketball Association's fine coaches, on why he removed three of his finest players at a critical point in a playoff game: "When the ball went up, we didn't want to be rebounding with conscientious objectors."

Coach **BILL FITCH**, assessing his Cleveland Cavaliers squad: "We're so slow, we had three loose balls roll dead in practice the other day."

ROD HUNDLEY, former NBA great and now a TV sportscaster, recalling how he signed as a first-round NBA draft choice in 1957 for a $10,000 salary and no bonus: "Every time I see my mother I say, 'Why didn't you wait?'"

GEORGE RAVELLING, one of America's finest collegiate basketball coaches, after hearing the Arizona coach complain about the problems involved in traveling to the Northwest: "It never bothered Lewis and Clark."

DIGGER PHELPS, Notre Dame basketball coach, announcing that the University of Indiana's sometimes fiery and highly successful basketball coach, **BOBBY KNIGHT**, was embarking on a new venture into the furniture business: "You buy a couch and he throws in a chair."

RICK COLLINS, preparatory school basketball coach, evaluating his team's chances: "We have a great bunch of outside shooters. Unfortunately all of our games are played indoors."

PAT WILLIAMS, Orlando Magic general manager, to reporters after head coach **MATT GOUKAS** failed to appear at a press conference announcing his hiring as coach: "I can understand your frustration. In college, I took 'Introduction to Shakespeare' and the guy never showed the whole semester."

Said **BILL FRIEDER**, then-Michigan basketball coach, after the Wolverines returned from the Great Alaska Shoot out in Fairbanks, Alaska: "We're never going back there. I don't care if we make the Final Four and if it's in Alaska, we're not going. Take a blizzard, no visibility, clouds—and that's Alaska 365 days a year. It amazes me some people live there, but they must like to drink."

ED MURPHY, Mississippi basketball coach, on why he started 6'–11" redshirt freshman **SEAN MURPHY**, his son, at center: "Because his mother wants it that way."

DANNY AINGE, former Boston Celtics star who is now with the Portland Trail Blazers, claiming that his reputation as a complainer is undeserved: "Actually, I'm not a complainer. I'm a whiner."

Outstanding NBA forward **DICK VAN ARSDALE** was playing with the Phoenix Suns in 1969 when his coach, **JOHNNY KERR**, told him that the team might make a trade with the Cincinnati Royals for Van Arsdale's twin brother, Tom. "Terrific," Dick said. "Who are you thinking of giving up for him?" Back shot the answer. "You."

After Utah Jazz center **MARK EATON** had been injured jumping for a ball, **BOB FORD** observed in the Philadelphia *Inquirer*: "Now why would he go and try that after all these years?"

University of Oregon Athletic Director **BILL BYRNE**, on the qualities he seeks in his search for a new basketball coach: "I want him to be able to walk on water and not scare the fish."

DENNIS RODMAN, Detroit Pistons star, asked if he would kiss **MAGIC JOHNSON** on the cheek before a game like **ISAIAH THOMAS** did: "I think we should get engaged first."

FRANK LAYDEN, former Utah Jazz coach, who in addition to his great basketball knowledge was renowned as an outstanding storyteller, relating an experience about weighing himself: "I stepped on a scale that gives fortune cards and the card read, 'Come back in fifteen minutes—alone.'"

PAT WILLIAMS, general manager of the Orlando Magic, introducing NBA announcer and former NBA Coach **HUBIE BROWN** at a banquet: "Hubie was to network basketball ratings what the Titanic was to winter cruise business."

Former North Carolina State basketball coach **JIM VAL-VANO**: "We've been getting better rebounding,, but mostly we're rebounding our own missed shots."

MYCHAL THOMPSON of the Los Angeles Lakers, on the difference from the year he played for the Portland Trail Blazers: "This year I feel like the United States going against Libya. Last year I felt like Libya."

DEAN SMITH, North Carolina basketball coach: "If you make every game a life-and-death proposition, you're going to have problems. For one thing, you'll be dead a lot."

GEORGE RAVELING, Washington State basketball coach, on life in the Northwest: "I won't say it's remote up here but my last speech was featured in *Field and Stream*.

DIGGER PHELPS, Notre Dame basketball coach, asked by old graduate **CARL YASTREMSKI**, Boston Red Sox star, when his team was finally going to win a championship: "Funny, I was going to ask you the same question."

SHELBY METCALF, basketball coach at Texas A&M, recounting what he told a player who received four F's and one D on his report card: "Son, looks to me like you're spending too much time on one subject."

DETLEF SCHREMPF, German Olympic basketball star, after it was announced that the Phoenix Suns would play in an exhibition tournament in Munich: "I hope they don't let **CHARLES**

BARKLEY get a taste of our German beer. If he gets into that, we could have a problem."

Center **DAVID ROBINSON**, finishing his U.S. Navy commitment at Kings Bay, Georgia, before joining the San Antonio Spurs of the NBA: "I know I have the potential to be one of the best players in the world, and that's an incredible thing to think about when you're sitting behind a desk."

After the Boston Celtics worst loss of the season, 119-84, to the Houston Rockets, Boston Celtics forward **KEVIN McHALE** was asked if he would be retiring: "If I was going to retire, I wouldn't do it in the Houston locker room after a ninety-eight point loss."

JIM VALVANO, former North Carolina State basketball coach, admitting he's a cable TV sports junkie: "I don't go to sleep until midget tag team wrestling comes on."

Basketball star **CHARLES BARKLEY** on Tonya Harding calling herself the Charles Barkley of figure skating: "I was going to sue her for defamation of character, but then I realized that I have no character."

BILL RUSSELL, Boston Celtics center, on why his father couldn't retire: "He said he had given the company thirty good years of his life, and now he wants to give them a few bad ones."

Former L.A. Lakers basketball coach **PAT RILEY**: "I told our players when **KAREEM** leaves, I'll finally get a chance to see if they're any good. One of them looked at me and said. 'Okay, and we'll see if you can really coach.'"

During an exchange of experiences while attending high school, **FRANK LAYDEN**, Utah Jazz coach and humorist, told of the high school he graduated from in Brooklyn: "Boy, was it tough. We had nicknames like Rocky, Scarface, Rat Head, and Toothless—and they were just the cheerleaders."

DIGGER PHELPS, coach of Notre Dame, on the advantage of having a father who was an undertaker: "When I was dating my wife, I could send her flowers every day."

AL McGUIRE, outstanding former basketball coach, during a college game: "In a time-out, when my players said they understood a play I designed, I knew they didn't."

"HOT ROD" HUNDLEY, NBA great, relating his biggest basketball thrill: "It was the night that **ELGIN BAYLOR** and I combined for seventy-five points—Elgin had seventy-one of them."

BOB BASS, making an observation about an opposing team's center: "He was in the three-second lane longer than Smokey the Bear has been in the woods."

AL McGUIRE, upon hearing that **RICK MAJERUS,** Marquette's basketball coach, had lost twenty pounds: "Rick Majerus losing twenty pounds is like the Queen Mary losing a deck chair."

NORM SLOAN, on why he can't stand teams that play zone defense: "It looks like a stick-up at a 7-Eleven store with five tall guys holding their hands in the air."

In their playing days in the National Basketball Association (NBA), both the Boston Celtics' great center **BILL RUSSELL** and the equally great Philadelphia 76er's pivot man **WILT CHAMBERLAIN** were renowned as fierce competitors and more so when they played against one another. Russell was once asked why Chamberlain didn't have a high percentage in foul shooting. Said Russell: "Even if I'd known why he couldn't shoot foul shots, I'd never have told him."

PAT KENNEDY, Iona basketball coach, asked whether North Carolina's height advantage accounted for a forty-three point defeat: "When you're hit by an avalanche who has time to measure the boulders?"

ALEXANDER WOLFF, on why referee Tony Nunez was called "Mascara" in the NBA: "Because he makes so many make-up calls."

PETE GILLEN, on being basketball coach at Xavier University in Cincinnati: "I'm just a caraway seed in the bakery of life."

BUTCH VON BREDA KOLFF, on why he prefers to coach basketball on the women's level: "Because of the time-outs—they smell better."

RICKY GRACE, Oklahoma basketball star, on his chronic hand injury: "It's been frozen and defrosted more than a pork chop."

Brigham Young's 7'6" center **SHAWN BRADLEY**, when asked whether he's self-conscious about his height: "I love being 7'6". I wouldn't trade it for anything. I was taught to have self-esteem and have a good positive attitude about myself." Asked about dancing with women under six feet tall, Bradley said: "I stand them on a chair. If people start to have fun and make fun of it, that's their problem."

Boston Celtic forward **KEVIN McHALE**, on the resurgence of his teammate, point guard **JOHN BAGLEY**: "The only person who's had a bigger comeback than Bagley is Lazarus."

Campbell University basketball coach **BILLY LEE**, on the news the Camels would play top-ranked Duke in the first round of the NCAA Tournament: "We're going to a sword fight with a toothpick."

ESPN's **JOHN SAUNDERS** after Brigham Young's **KEVIN NIXON** "stole" the WAC Tournament title from Texas-El Paso with a fifty-four foot shot at the buzzer: "Turns out that Nixon is, in fact, a crook."

MICHAEL JORDAN, Chicago Bulls basketball star: "The game is my wife. It demands loyalty and responsibility and it gives me back fulfillment and peace."

PAT RILEY, telling reporters it no longer bothers him he has never been voted NBA coach of the year: "Besides I get more credit for not getting enough credit than any man in the history of the game. So what the hell!"

It was reported that Celtic's star **LARRY BIRD**, when in Madrid with the Boston Celtics, went to Spain's largest department store, El Cortes Ingles, and signed 2,200 autographs in sixty-five minutes. "I signed until my hand gave out," said Bird after breaking the store record for signing autographs, a record set by **SOPHIA LOREN**. That means he signed his name every 1.8 seconds. Is that possible?

PAT WILLIAMS, general manager of the Orlando Magic, describing his job: "It's like a nervous breakdown with a weekly paycheck."

RALPH MILLER, Oregon State basketball coach, talking about his ranked team a few years ago: "This is some bunch. I can't even show them game films of themselves. All they do is clap."

BRAD DAUGHERTY, Cleveland Cavs center, on guarding Michael Jordan: "When he takes it to the basket, three things can happen. You're either going to foul him, or he's going to score, or you foul him while he's scoring."

Boston Celtics coach **K.C. JONES**, when asked about the injury situation: "If I see guys on crutches, with bandages on their head, and someone's playing a fife and drum, I'll know I'm in trouble."

From **PHIL JACKMAN** of the Baltimore *Evening Sun*: "With each passing Washington Bullets defeat, I am reminded of what team general manager **BOB FERRY** said during training camp: 'We're continually looking to improve at every position.' How about at general manager?"

TOMMY CANTERBURY, Centenary basketball coach: "The trouble with officials is that they don't care who wins."

JOHN KERR, former National League star and coach of the East team in an NBA Old-Timers game in Chicago: "My job is to be sure everyone gets to all of the parties."

Former basketball coach and TV announcer **AL McGUIRE** on his coaching style at Marquette: "I wanted my teams to have my personality—surly, obnoxious, and arrogant."

BENNY DEES, basketball coach at Alabama, on how he turned down high school star **CHARLES BARKLEY** while recruiting for the Crimson Tide: "I figured he'd gain forty pounds and become a slob. Instead he gained eighty pounds and became a superstar."

Basketball star **MARVIN "BAD NEWS" BARNES**, when he was playing for the St. Louis Spirits of the old American Basketball Association, reported forty-five minutes late for practice one day, and coach **ROD THORN** wondered why. "Car trouble," Barnes said. "Didn't you just buy a new Rolls Royce?" Thorn asked. Replied Barnes; "Yeah, but they just don't make 'em like they used to."

DARRELL GRIFFITH, Louisville basketball star, about the No. 11 worn by 7'3" Soviet center Vladmir Tkachenko before the Cardinals lost to the U.S.S.R. National Team 91–76: "It looks like a pair of expressways running down his shirt."

TODD PHIPERS of the Denver *Post*: "Which is going to come first for **BOB KNIGHT**, cardiac arrest or just arrest?"

When Boston Celtic star **KEVIN McHALE** was lost to the team due to foot injury, the Celtics were otherwise intact with **LARRY BIRD** and **ROBERT PARISH** up front and **DENNIS JOHNSON** and **DANNY AINGE** in the back court. Said Johnson: "With Kevin out, Robert will see the ball more. No doubt he'll score. But this team is rather odd. When Kevin goes down, Danny thinks he has the option of shooting ten more times. Larry thinks that way and Robert thinks that way. I told them I think that way too, but I've got the ball."

ABE LEMONS, Oklahoma City University coach, on why coaching is tougher than practicing medicine: "Doctors bury their mistakes. We still have ours on scholarship."

Auburn basketball coach **SONNY SMITH**, on Alabama coach **WIMP SANDERSON** and his dour countenance: "I read where it takes fifteen muscles to smile and sixty-five muscles to frown, so I figure that Wimp is suffering from muscle fatigue."

WILT CHAMBERLAIN, great NBA center, inducted into the San Pedro (California) Sportswalk at age fifty-one, after a suggestion that Chamberlain could still make mincemeat of some NBA centers: "They are mincemeat."

Miami Heat basketball coach **RON ROTHSTEIN**: "Our nine-through-twelve people are probably as good or better than anybody else in the league. It's one-through-eight where you have the problem."

Wrote **PHIL JACKMAN** of the Baltimore *Evening Sun*: "**MIKE FRATELLO**, coach of the Atlanta Hawks basketball team that played three games with the Russians before the Olympics, offered **JOHN THOMPSON** (coach of the Olympic team) a scouting report on the Russians but Thompson refused it."

ANDREW GAZE, a native Australian who once played for the number ten-rated Seton Hall basketball team, said in a live radio interview back home, "We're doing very well, we're in the top ten." There was a silence from down-under. "They didn't understand at first," Glaze told *Newsday*. "Back home, there are only fourteen schools."

Boston Celtics star guard **DENNIS JOHNSON** was going to be invited to be on the board of trustees of the Eugene V. Debs School of Activism. Asked how he became the Celtics' player representative, Johnson shrugged and said, "I don't know. I guess I was the last guy to come into the room that night."

Former NBA player and coach **JOHNNY KERR**, on coaching: "If a coach starts listening to the fans, he winds up sitting next to them."

BOBBY KNIGHT, asked by **DICK VITALE** during an ESPN interview if he had ever done anything he regretted: "Yeah. Back in 1968, I was the coach of the Army (West Point) team, and we were playing Notre Dame in the NIT Tournament in New York, and at half time I could have done a better job of coaching."

When the Boston Celtics great center **DAVE COWENS** was announcing his retirement, he gave an eloquent and inspiring good-bye to his teammates aboard the team bus during an exhibition season swing through Indiana. He told them he enjoyed playing with them but that, because of various ailments, it wouldn't be fair to them or the public if he tried to continue. The news was greeted by a hushed silence finally broken uproariously, when Celtic guard **M.L. CARR** shouted, "Then get the hell off our bus."

Former Cleveland Cavalier basketball coach **LENNY WILKINS**, on the easygoing manner of NBA great **WILT CHAMBERLAIN**: "There are a lot of guys walking around today because Wilt didn't lose his temper."

National Basketball Association star **CHARLES BARKLEY** on the inauguration of **PRESIDENT GEORGE BUSH:** "I voted for George Bush. My family got all over me because they said Bush is only for the rich people. Then I reminded them, 'Hey, I am rich.'"

DENNIS JOHNSON, Boston Celtics star guard, was watching on TV when little brother **CRAIG**, 5'7" guard for Grand Canyon College, made a spectacular block during the team's 88–86 win over Auburn Montgomery in the NA championship game. Announcer **DICK VITALE** started screaming, "Dennis Johnson is home in his apartment jumping up right now." After reading Vitale's remark in the newspaper, D.J. said, "That's the most amazing thing. I did exactly what Vitale said I was doing. That's pretty good timing."

When Indiana basketball fans threw coins on the floor to protest a couple of technical calls against coach **BOBBY KNIGHT** during a game against Michigan State at Assembly Hall in Bloomington, Indiana, Knight, who once tossed a chair across the basketball court at Assembly Hall, grabbed the microphone and admonished the fans. "Keep in mind we don't throw things here," Knight said, "I don't care what the quality of officiating is, we don't throw anything here."

From **SPEEDY MORRIS**, LaSalle College basketball coach: "When I first got the job at LaSalle, the phone rang and my wife told me it was *Sports Illustrated*. I cut myself shaving and fell down the stairs in my rush to get to the phone. And when I got there, a voice on the other end said, 'For just seventy-five cents an issue....'"

ANDREW LANG of the Phoenix Suns and his wife, Bronwyd, who met while both played basketball at the University of Arkansas, were expecting their first child. Bronwyd Lang had a better shooting percentage in college than her husband, a 6'11" center. Said Sun Coach **COTTON FITZSIMMONS**: "I'd sure like to have the draft rights to that baby."

JEFF RULAND, center for the NBA's Philadelphia 76ers, on missing more than one hundred games over a two-year span, despite committing himself to weight lifting, reducing his alcoholic intake, and improving his eating habits: "I never had these problems when I drank a lot and stuffed my face with Polish sausages."

BILL LAIMBEER of the Detroit Pistons, on his fine of $5,000 for body-slamming Boston Celtics star **LARRY BIRD** during a game in Boston: "All it means is that my wife will get a potted plant instead of a diamond necklace for our anniversary in August."

When NBA basketball great **JULIUS ERVING** was honored before his last game in Chicago Stadium, **JOHNNY KERR**, a former NBA center who was the Chicago Bull's announcer, was the master of ceremonies. Said Kerr: "This man had an illustrious high school career, an illustrious college career, and an illustrious career in the pros. But enough about me."

KAREEN ABDUL-JABBAR, great center for the Los Angeles Lakers, on the power of Boston Celtics pride and tradition: "They didn't buy all those banners at Woolworth's."

Former Philadelphia 76ers coach **GENE SHUE**, when he was coach of the Los Angeles Clippers, recalling a closed-door meeting in which he "read out" the players for leaking stories to the press: "Fifteen minutes after I told them that, one of the sportswriters had the story."

It has become popular for National Basketball Association players to wear those nylon shorts under game shorts, and technically the reason is the shorts keep hamstring muscles warm. But that is not the only reason. Some players say they wear them to be fashionable. Dallas Mavericks forward **ADRIAN DANTLEY** says he accepts neither reason. "The only reason guys wear them is because they have a fat butt or their thighs aren't really toned," Dantley said. "It's just like a lady wearing a girdle."

Denver Nugget coach **DOUG MOE**, asked what he thought of being named coach of the All-Interview team as chosen by NBA writers: "No comment."

JIM LYNAM, when he was coaching the NBA's San Diego Clippers, was asked by the writers to stop replying to their questions with one-word answers. "Why?" Lynam said. Later, when he was the coach of the Philadelphia 76ers, and a Philadelphia *Daily News* writer asked him if that actually happened. Lynam thought for a moment. "True," he said.

After **BILL RUSSELL** and the Boston Celtics had beaten **WILT CHAMBERLAIN** and the Los Angeles Lakers in the 1968–69 NBA championship series, **JERRY WEST** was asked who was the better center. West, of the Lakers, had been named the MVP of the series. Said West: "I think Wilt Chamberlain is a better basketball player than Bill Russell, but for the one game, I think I'd rather have Bill Russell. It would be hard to explain without hurting someone's feelings. I think Chamberlain is a better rebounder, a better scorer, and a better shooter, but if I had to pick one guy for one game, it'd be Russell. It's incredible what he does for his team. It's hard to imagine how one guy can do so much for his teammates. When you see them on the court, they're different players. I can't think of any guy, in any sport, in any time that has dominated his game the way Russell has. I think the players in the NBA respect him most of any player."

Now-it-can-be-told department: When **RICK CARLISLE** signed with the New York Knicks, his former Boston Celtic teammate **BILL WALTON** sent him a congratulatory telegram from Baja,

California, where Walton was recuperating from foot surgery. Walton sent the entire telegram in Spanish.

Washington Bullets forward **DON MacLEAN** was known more for his scoring than for his defensive prowess. After he became involved in a brawl while defending a girlfriend, one of ESPN's basketball announcers remarked: "That's the first person he has defended all year."

When rookie guard **REX CHAPMAN** of the Charlotte Hornets was at the University of Kentucky, some observers were comparing him with Hall of Famer **JERRY WEST**. Said super scout **MARTY BLAKE**: "If I had $100 for every 'next Jerry West' I've seen, I could have retired long ago. I think Chapman would do well to be the next Danny Ainge."

DARRELL WALKER wasn't happy about his trade from the Denver Nuggets to the Washington Bullets. Said Walker: "Washington, of all the places. Washington! All that banging and hitting and pushing and shoving and fighting. I'll be throwing the ball to Moses (Malone) and Bernard (King). Won't be anymore thirty-point nights for me."

ALAN GREENBERG of the Hartford Courant, on the champagne in the Los Angeles Lakers dressing room: "The brand was Cook's, $2.00 a bottle at your local Los Angeles supermarket." He added: "The Lakers sprayed it and poured it over everyone, especially coach Pat Riley. Except for team captain **KAREEN ABDUL-JABBAR** who always manages to be a little different. He poured Hawaiian Punch."

DAVE GAVITT, when commissioner of the Big East Conference, told Joe Gergen of *Newsday* what it was like to play for coach **AL McGUIRE** when Gavitt was a freshman at Dartmouth College. "Al was then like the Al now," Gavitt said of McGuire, who went on to win a National Collegiate Athletic Association title at Maruqette in 1977. "He didn't know anyone's name. I was working like hell for two or three games, to get into the starting lineup, and we had a big game against Holy Cross. I must have hit seven of eight jump shots, and when he pulled me out of the game, he gave me a slap on the back and said 'Good job, George.'"

As is usually the case, boasting was the order of the day on NBA draft picks. Cleveland's **RANDOLPH KEYS** was compared with **BOB DANDRIDGE**, **MIKE MITCHELL**, and, potentially, **ALEX**

ENGLISH. Golden State coach Don Nelson called **MITCH RICH-MOND** "star quality" while Sacramento coach Jerry Richards said **RICKY BERRY** was the "player we wanted all along." But the best of all was Miami General Manger Lew Schaffel on **RONY SEIKALY**: "He's the people's choice. It's obvious Rony Seikaly is not only the player we wanted but the person South Florida wanted to have."

The year Alabama-Birmingham State beat defending champion Connecticut in the National Invitational Tournament no one was more impressed than St. John's coach **LOU CARNESECCA.** "When you beat Connecticut at their home court in Storrs, Connecticut, it's like beating the Russians in Moscow," Carnesecca said; "Napoleon couldn't win up there."

Said 6'11" **CHRIS DUDLEY** of the Cleveland Cavaliers after four of his shots had been blocked by 7'7" **MANUTE BOL** of the Washington Bullets: "The guy doesn't jump, you can't fake him because he just stands there with his hands up in the air. I've never seen anybody that big in my life."

When **MOSES MALONE** was playing for the Washington Bullets, he was asked if he would have a farewell tour around the league like superstar **JULIUS ERVING'S** when he retires. Said Moses: "Naw, I'm going to retire by telephone and ask them to mail in the gifts."

Nothing against Boston Celtics guard **DENNIS JOHNSON**, but National Basketball Association fans can only hope he doesn't last as long as **KAREEM ABDUL-JABBAR**. The reason? Every year in the league, Johnson has added one bounce to his ritual before taking a free (foul) shot. He was up to twelve bounces at the time. He admits to having second thoughts over his habit of taking all those bounces before making the throw. Said Johnson: "The other night, I was bouncing the ball six times. You do get pretty tired doing it twelve times."

MYCHAL THOMPSON of the Los Angeles Lakers, after the Boston Celtics had won a key game in the NBA championship final round: "I think everybody was secretly pulling for Boston to win for obvious reasons." (Pause) "Boston has the best clam chowder in the world."

NAT GOTTLIEB of the Newark *Star Ledger*, on New York Knicks forward **BILL CARTWRIGHT**: "In a league where height is so essential, it seems almost unjust that Bill Cartwright should be seven feet tall. Better he should be made to donate the extra foot he doesn't use to a worthy cause like **SPUD WEBB**, a guy with heart who would know what to do with the extra inches."

When California State University Hornets basketball team joined the Great Northern Conference, which stretched all the way to Anchorage, Alaska, some creative scheduling was necessary. The last home game for the Hornets was January 1st. After that they were off for ten days before finishing up their schedule with eight straight games on the road in the north territory. Said coach **JOE ANDERS**: "January was a great month to be a Hornet. February is a great month to be a Hornet travel agent."

Cleveland Cavaliers center **BRAD DAUGHERTY** was asked which NBA All-Star impressed him the most. "Moses Malone," he said, "because he always works hard, and I really admire that in a guy sixty years old."

From U.S. Senator **BILL BRADLEY**, D-N.J., former great Princeton and National Basketball Association All-Star: "How shall we Democrats choose our next presidential candidate? Shall it be in a smoke-filled room? Shall it be by brokered convention? Shall it be by a national primary? Personally I prefer jump shots from the top of the keypost."

In recent practices, Boston Celtic backup center **GREG KITE** collided with teammate **MARK ACRES,** bruising the rookie's left leg. He also elbowed **FRED ROBERTS** in the mouth, and when he caught **LARRY BIRD** with an elbow, coach K.C. Jones stopped practice. In a recent game, Kite stepped on Atlanta's **DOMINIQUE WILKINS** twice. Said Wilkins: "When he stepped on me the first time, it was like his foot was never going to move. After the second time, I said: 'This guy is lethal.'"

TONY KORNHEISER of the Washington *Post*: "The Washington Bullets are at least three players away from being a contender, and two of them are **MICHAEL JORDAN** and **PATRICK EWING**."

NEIL WILLIAMSON of Radio Station WQXI in Atlanta, after the Atlanta Hawks drafted 7'7", 320-pound **JORGE GONZALES** of Argentina: "He's a guy you don't want to bring up the Falkland War with."

Basketball coach **GEORGE RAVELING**, on sports writers: "The best years of their lives are spent in third grade."

PAT WILLIAMS, general manager of the Orlando Magic, on NBA Commissioner **DAVID STERN**, who was given a $27 million contract by NBA owners: "One of David's sons asked his father to buy him a chemistry set, and he went out and bought him DuPont."

When **HAKEEM OLAJHWON**, center of the Houston Rockets, sat out eight games because of iron deficiency anemia, **PETE CHILCUTT**, Houston Rocket forward/center, was asked how his absence affected the team: "It's like playing golf without the driver, "he said.

BRYANT "BIG COUNTRY" REEVES, Oklahoma State's 7', 292-pound star, possesses one of sports' best nicknames. Back when he was a freshman at OSU, direct from a small town, Gans, Oklahoma (population 346), Reeves, on his first airplane flight, reportedly told a flight attendant that because of the plane's cabin pressure, his ears were bothering him. She suggested that some chewing gum might help. The story goes that Big Country peeled the wrapper off a stick of gum and stuck it in his ear.

When **WAYNE BOULTINGHOUSE** was basketball coach of Indiana State-Evansville, he spoke of the advantages of having 7' 6 1/2" center **JOHN HOLLINDEN**: "Just the other day we were in the Atlanta airport and John helped out one of his teammates by reaching over the doors of the pay toilets and opening them from the inside."

TOMMY VARDEMAN, assistant basketball coach at Louisiana's Centenary College, on bench warmers: "Every team needs huggers. Those are the guys you sign up so you can hug 'em after you win, instead of having to hug the guys who play and sweat."

PETER SALZBERG, University of Vermont basketball coach, after three Southwest Conference officials assessed fifty-six fouls during Vermont's 98–66 loss at Texas A & M: "They called fouls like they were getting a commission."

GEORGE RAVELING, Washington State basketball coach, one of the few blacks coaching a major college team: "When the athletic director said I should recruit more white players to keep the folks in Pullman (Washington) happy, I signed Rufus White and Willie White."

DENNY CRUM, Louisville University basketball coach, on his contract: "I'm getting $300,000, but over a 150-year period."

BILLY PAULTZ, on the adjustment he had to make after being traded from the San Antonio Spurs to his new team, the Houston Rockets: "The warm-up pants here have snaps. That's more complicated than the offense."

DARRELL HEDRIC, Miami of Ohio basketball coach, after his team lost to Purdue 76–57: "If you want to know the turning point, it was our lay-up drill."

MIKE OWENS, teammate of the University of Virginia's 7'4" **RALPH SAMPSON**: "People keep coming up to Ralph and asking him if he's Ralph Sampson. I mean, who else could he be?"

DANA KIRK, Mempis State basketball coach, who provided the TV commentary for a game in which **LES HENSON**'s eighty-nine foot desperation shot at the buzzer gave Virginia Tech a 79–77 victory over Florida State: "Quite frankly I thought he took a bad shot."

BILL FITCH, former Boston Celtic coach: "I don't have an ulcer. I'm a carrier. I give them to other people."

ABE LEMON, University of Texas basketball coach, after punishing his players by telling them they couldn't return to their hotel in Abilene until 10 P.M.: "It was Sunday night and everything was shut down...I'd be doing them a favor by letting them come in early."

RICH KELLEY, journeyman NBA center, who received a standing ovation from Phoenix (Arizona) fans following his trade to the Suns from the New Jersey Nets: "Give them time. They'll learn."

REGGIE THEUS, one of the three Chicago Bull guards—the others are **RICKY SOBERS** and **SAM SMITH**—from Nevada-Las Vegas: "If we get one more player from Nevada-Las Vegas, the National Basketball Association will put us on probation."

MARVIN BARNES, Boston Celtic forward, on how he managed to earn so many college credits while he was serving time in prison: "There was no place I could go to cut classes."

WALT FRAZIER, recalling his trade years ago from the New York Knickerbockers to the Cleveland Cavaliers: "The people who were the sorriest were my tailor, my furrier, and my shoemaker."

LYNN WHEELER, after resigning as the coach of Iowa State's women's basketball team, which finished the season with fourteen straight defeats: "I've taken this team as far as I can."

Boxer MUHAMMAD ALI, asked why NBA basketball star WILT CHAMBERLAIN never changed his name: "He wanted to, but the one he wanted was taken—BILL RUSSELL."

When HORACE GRANT of the Chicago Bulls was at Clemson, he was asked if he was interested in talking to ALAN WILLIAMS of Princeton, who beat him out for best field-goal percentage in the nation. Said Grant: "The only phone number I want from Princeton is BROOKE SHIELDS."

Broadcaster BOB COSTAS, on the multi-colored sports coat of Alabama basketball coach WIMP SANDERSON: "It's good to see that PINKY LEE'S estate has been settled."

Certainly MICHAEL JORDAN turned the Chicago Bulls around, but it wasn't too long ago that the team was in disarray. In the pre-Jordan days, MAGIC JOHNSON had this to say after learning that ANN LANDERS attended the Bull's games at Chicago Stadium: "She must have problems of her own."

MANUTE BOL, 7' 7" center of the Washington Bullets, about female companionship around the NBA circuit: "I tried American girls," he told JOHN EISENBERG of the Baltimore *Sun* "but they talk too much." Bol married a 5' 11", nineteen-year-old woman named ATONG, in the city of Khartoum. For her dowry, he gave her eighty cows. "She is more my kind," Bol said. "She is quiet. I like quiet girls." Note: If the marriage doesn't work out, Bol gets the cows back.

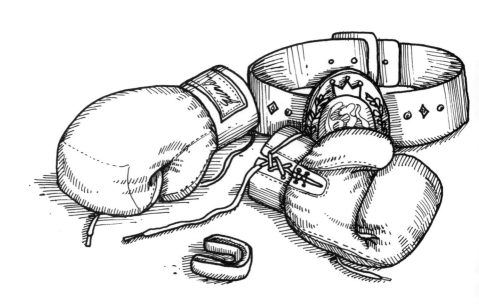

PART 3

FOOTBALL

A Brief History

American football evolved in the nineteenth century as a combination of rugby and soccer. The first intercollegiate football match in the United States is usually credited to the game played in 1869 by Princeton University and Rutgers College at New Brunswick, New Jersey, but that game more resembled the kicking style of association football (soccer) than modern football: there were twenty-five players on a team, and the game was won by the number of goals scored rather than by touchdowns. In 1873, the first collegiate rules were standardized by Princeton, Columbia, Rutgers, and Yale, and soon afterward the distinct American version of football began to develop.

The innovations of sports authority Walter Camp were fundamental in the evolution of American football. In 1880, Camp substituted the scrimmage for the rugby scrum, initiated the dominant role of the quarterback, and reduced the number of players on a team from fifteen to eleven. He established the standard formations now used and introduced systems for scoring and measuring downs and yards gained. Tackling rules were also liberalized. Rules were created that included the introduction of the forward pass, new formations, and the prohibition of blocking with extended arms.

In 1910, the National Collegiate Athletic Association (NCAA) was formed to govern American intercollegiate competition. Post Season or "bowl" games played between leading college teams became popular and now include the Rose Bowl (Pasadena, California), the Orange Bowl (Miami, Florida), the Sugar Bowl (New Orleans, Louisiana), the Sun Bowl (El Paso, Texas), the Cotton Bowl (Dallas, Texas), and the Gator Bowl (Jacksonville, Florida).

Sports Quotes and Anecdotes

FOOTBALL

Football coach **SANDY BUDA**, on the rash of injuries that hit his Nebraska-Omaha team: "We have so many guys in the whirlpool, that the only way to get them out to practice is to play the theme song from *Jaws*."

LOU HOLTZ, after the three men involved in hiring him at Notre Dame (Fr. Theodore Hesburgh, President Fr; Edmund Joyce, Executive V.P.; and Gene Corrigan, Athletic Director) left their positions: "In my first month on the job, all three announced they were leaving. I started calling home every three hours to see if my wife had left."

LOU HOLTZ, Notre Dame football coach, when his team was pelted with oranges after earning a trip to the Orange Bowl: "I'm just glad we're not going to the Gator Bowl."

DOUG VANCE, University of Kansas sports information director, after the football team bus hit the wing of a parked plane at the Montgomery, Alabama, airport: "Looks like we'll be going to the single wing offense."

Former Notre Dame and Green Bay Packers back **PAUL HORNUNG**, on **DICK BUTKUS**: "Dick would not only tackle you, he would consume you."

REGGIE WILLIAMS, Cincinnati Bengal linebacker, on his attributes: "Speed, strength, and the ability to recognize pain immediately."

JOHN McKAY, former Tampa Bay Buccaneer coach, on his mail: "It's about three to one I'm not a S.O.B.; but there are a lot of ones."

Chicago Bears coach **MIKE DITKA** when asked what quarterback **JIM McMAHON** was doing to rehabilitate his shoulder said: "He's hitting the five-iron about one hundred and eighty yards."

RON LUCIANO, former major league umpire, a 1958 Syracuse University graduate who was drafted by the Detroit Lions as an offensive lineman: "I played tackle in college but I was too small for the pros. After my first year with the Lions I went to coach **GEORGE WILSON** and told him that I really enjoyed playing under him, and I wanted him to put me wherever I could help the club most.

He took me up on it and two weeks later I was traded to Minnesota. What a great sense of humor that man had."

MACK BROWN, new North Carolina football coach, asked his toughest assignment since taking the job: "Getting **J.R. REIDS'** autograph for my eleven-year-old daughter."

ALEX KARRAS, Detroit Lions defensive tackle, on his golf game: "My best score ever was 103 but I've only been playing for 15 years."

Houston Mayor **JIM McCONN** on Houston Oilers great running back **EARL CAMPBELL**: "He ought to run for president, because if he runs for mayor, he'll beat me."

KEN PAYNE, former Philadelphia Eagle wide receiver, when told a woman sportswriter was in the dressing room: "Uh, oh! I'd better put my teeth in."

MONTE CLARK, Detroit Lions coach, on **LARRY CSONKA**, All Pro full-back: "When he goes on safari, the lions roll up their windows."

Nebraska football coach **TOM OSBORNE**, recalling his two-year stint as an end for the Washington Redskins: "We had an incentive pay system. You got money for such things as yards, completions, fumble recoveries, and interceptions. When we added it all together, I owed the team $34.50."

JACK KEMP, prominent Republican figure and former pro quarterback: "Pro football gave me a good perspective when I entered the political arena. I had already been booed, cheered, cut, sold, traded, and hung in effigy."

University of Washington football coach **DON JAMES**, on why he wasn't thinking of retiring as rumored: "I've got a daughter that I've got to get through college and I've got a wife who is a world class shopper."

Notre Dame football coach **LOU HOLTZ** on his youth: "You hear people talk about having an inferiority complex. Me, I didn't have a complex; frankly I was inferior."

BUM PHILLIPS, former Houston Oilers coach, when asked if the acquisition of Oakland quarterback **KEN STABLER** would put the Oilers in the Super Bowl: "Yep, if we win more games than anybody else."

TIM SALEM, a freshman quarterback at Minnesota, where his father, **JOE**, is coach: "The other day I ran out of money, so I asked Coach for $5. He told me I'm a player now and the rules don't permit a coach to give a college player money."

LARRY KENNAN, Lamar University football coach, after Baylor University attempted an onside kick with eight seconds left and a 42–7 lead: "Maybe they were afraid we'd run it all the way back, then line up and go for thirty points."

JIM BAKKEN, former St. Louis Cardinals place-kicker, at a dinner "roasting" St. Louis' 280-pound guard **BOB YOUNG**: "For his salad, you just pour vinegar and oil on your lawn and let him graze."

Former All Pro lineman **CONRAD DOBLER** on the National Football League's czar **PETE ROZELLE**: "I've always had a hard time trusting someone with a year-round tan who lives in New York."

Defensive end **DEXTER MANLEY** of the Washington Redskins, complaining that he is constantly being held: "If I were the football commissioner, all offensive linemen guilty of holding would get thirty days in jail or one week coached by **MIKE DITKA**."

BRUCE COSLET, former coach of the New York Jets, on free agency in the National Football League: "Its like recruiting for college, only the money is on the table instead of under it."

Iowa State football coach **JIM WALDEN**, on Nebraska football teams: "I don't think there's much for Jim Walden to say that's not the same old boring stuff. They're big, they're strong, they're fast, their mothers love them, and what else? They have nice red suits and they have a nice white hat with a letter 'N' on it and they kill you."

Senior place-kicker **KURT DASBACH**, after missing a last minute, thirty-five yard field goal against Dartmouth that would have ended Columbia's record losing streak: "It felt good. I don't feel I choked. It was either the wind or the full moon or gravity or something."

CBS commentator **JOHN MADDEN** and announcer **VERN LUNDQUIST** bantered about measures players took to replace salt during games in hot weather. Said Madden: "I remember (former

Packer guard) Fuzzy Thurston trying to get some electrolytes." Said Lundquist: "They didn't have electric lights when Fuzzy Thurston played."

Miami Dolphin running back **SAMMY SMITH**, who promised each of his linemen a watch if Smith gained 1,300 yards this season: "If I only get 1,000 yards, they might only get Seikos instead of Rolexes."

Offensive tackle **JIM LACHEY**, on going from the San Diego Chargers to the Los Angeles Raiders to the Washington Redskins in a period of five weeks: "I'm just a rent-a-tackle. I go wherever there's a need."

Alabama football coach **BEAR BRYANT**: "When we had a good team at Alabama, I know it's because we have boys from good mamas and papas."

Former Atlanta Falcons football coach **MARION CAMP-BELL** once told **JERRY GREENE** of the Orlando *Sentinel*: "I think we've got the right kind of people to stay with it and win." Said Greene: "So did General Custer."

Former NFL linebacker **MATT MILLEN**, who reportedly had a tempestuous relationship with coach **JOE PATERNO** at Penn State, at a roast for the coach: "When you take off those glasses, does the nose come with them?"

JOHN McKAY, when asked about his team's execution when he was coach of the Tampa Bay Buccaneers: "I'm all for it."

Former assistant general manager of the Washington Redskins **BOBBY MITCHELL** said that the late **EDWARD BEN-NETT WILLIAMS**, a great courtroom orator, sometimes would give fight talks to the team. "It would work for one half," Mitchell said. "He was trying, but then someone like **ERNIE STAUTNER** (All Pro lineman) would hit you in the mouth, and you'd forget everything Williams said."

DAVE BUTZ of the Washington Redskins, on his hospitalization for food poisoning: "I was in so long the leaves changed on me."

Former Dallas Cowboys personnel director **GIL BRANDT** when asked to name the fastest football player ever: "I checked our files just to see which college player was the fastest ever timed at forty yards. It was **KIRK GIBSON**, then a wide receiver for Michigan State. He was timed in 4.31, faster than **BOB HAYES** (world class sprinter) ever did."

Penn State football coach **JOE PATERNO**, when asked what he thought of former Syracuse football coach **DICK MacPHERSON'S** calling him Machiavellian: "I'm surprised he knows what Machiavellian means."

DONNIE DUNCAN, Iowa State football coach, speaking about running back **MICHAEL WADE**, a high school quarter-mile champion: "I guess Wade is the man we'll turn to when it's third and a quarter-mile to go."

Former Pittsburgh Steeler great **JOE GREEN**, who wore all four of his Super Bowl rings on his right hand: "Our motto for next season is, 'One for the thumb in '81.'"

LARRY LACEWELL, Arkansas State football coach, after a senior quit, leaving the inexperienced team with three seniors and ten juniors: "Only thirteen more to go and we'll be a junior college."

CORBY SMITH, seven-year-old son of Arizona's new football coach **LARRY SMITH**, catching a look at the Wildcats' rugged 1980 schedule: "Gee, Dad, is that the real Notre Dame?"

Notre Dame linebacker **JEREMY NALI** asked to name his most memorable sporting event: "The egg toss in Cub Scouts."

LINDY INFANTE, coach of the Green Bay Packers: "I honestly feel there's a light at the end of the tunnel, and I don't think its simply a train anymore."

All Pro lineman **WILBUR MARSHALL**, on the difference between former coach **MIKE DITKA** at Chicago and new coach **JOE GIBBS** at Washington: "It's like night and day. You can't make the comparison. I talked to Gibbs, and he's the nicest man I ever met. I'm used to someone hollering and yelling."

GEORGE MacINTYRE, Vanderbilt football coach, recalling a recruiting trip last fall after his Commodores had been routed 66–3 by Alabama: "I told the recruits they had a chance to play for us right away, but I had a funny feeling they already knew that."

BUM PHILLIPS, Houston Oiler coach, offering words of wisdom to new acquisition HOLLYWOOD HENDERSON, who was getting what might have been his last chance in the NFL: "You don't know a ladder has splinters in it until you slide down it."

Former Detroit Lion tackle JOHN WOODCOCK walked out on the club as a result of a contract dispute. The Lions got their first clue that Woodcock was quitting when he failed to show up for scheduled treatment in the training room. They got their second clue when they found his football shoe in a garbage can. Coach MONTE CLARK later allowed, "I took that as a bad sign."

DAN McCANN, Duquesne University football coach, after being beaten 30–28 on a field goal by Georgetown U. Junior JIM CORCORAN, who had also beaten the Dukes with a field goal in 1978, and a punt-return touchdown in 1979: "I plan to attend his graduation."

Seattle Seahawks linebacker BRIAN BOSWORTH, on his slow recovery from a shoulder injury: "It's like shopping with your grandmother. You hurry up and wait."

DICK BUTKUS, All Pro lineman, denying he was a dirty football player: "I never set out to hurt anybody deliberately unless it was, you know, important—like a league game or something."

Iowa football coach HAYDEN FRY, on 6' 8" sophomore quarterback DAN McGUIRE, brother of Oakland Athletics slugger MARK McGUIRE: "He has the strongest arm of any professional, college, high school, or junior high school player I've ever seen. He can literally take one step and throw the ball ninety yards. The problem is we don't have anyone who can run fast enough to catch it."

Chicago Bears' coach MIKE DITKA, after TIM McGEE of the Cincinnati Bengals knocked him off his feet on a sideline play: "I'm sore. I can't take it anymore, guys. In the old days, I 'woulda moidered da bum.'"

Former L.A. Raiders coach TOM FLORES, recalling the ramshackled War Memorial Field in Buffalo, a far cry from the new 80,020 seat Rich Stadium the Bills moved into in 1973: "When I played for the Bills, I enjoyed that old stadium. I hear they're getting ready to tear it down and are bringing back all the famous people who played there." Flores paused. "They didn't invite me," he said.

Former Florida State football coach **BILL PETERSON**, who became a living legend with his malapropism and mixed metaphors. These are from a collection by **BILL McGROTHA** of the Tallahassee *Democrat*:

"I'm the football coach around here and don't you remember it."

"They gave me a standing observation."

"All we have to do is capitalize on our mistakes."

"Let's nip this thing in the butt."

"I couldn't remember things until I took that Sam Carnegie course."

Asked if he thought it would rain: "What do you think I am, a geologist?"

To the team captain before a game: "Lead us into a few words of silent prayer."

On his offense: "We're going to throw the ball, come hell or high water. We're not gonna be any three clouds-and-a-yard-of-dust team."

KEN DENLINGER of the Washington *Post*, on the Arena Football League, in which players get $500 a game: "It's pay scale might be less than most teams in the Southwest Conference."

Former Indianapolis Colts coach **RON MEYER**, who often led the NFL in malapropisms, with this response to criticism of **ERIC DICKERSON**: "Don't judge a book by the cover. Don't believe everything you read. There are always two sides to every story."

Two gems from the mouth of former Florida State football coach **BILL PETERSON**: "This is the greatest country in America." On being named to the Florida Hall of Fame: "I'm very appreciative of being indicted."

LAWRENCE TAYLOR of the New York Giants, who suffered a pulled hamstring muscle against the Philadelphia Eagles, and it occurred while he was chasing the Eagles quarterback **RANDALL CUNNINGHAM**: "He's got five gears. I ain't got but four."

Said Iowa State football coach **JIM WALDEN**, when asked about his team's chances against a very strong Oklahoma team: "Are you sadistic or what? I thought about not showing up, but what else can we do but play the game?"

Grambling College football coach **EDDIE ROBINSON** on why he chose to start 465 pound **RAYMOND "WORLD" SMITH**—

who because of his size was given a slim chance of making it in college football—when Grambling played Howard University: "He is a great pass blocker. And when he traps them, they stay trapped. When he leads a sweep, they get swept."

FRANK BROYLES, when he was Arkansas athletic director, on whether he'd still like his football coach, **KEN HATFIELD**, if the team won only half its games: "Sure I would. I'd miss him, too."

Miami Dolphins personnel director **CHARLEY WINNER**, on why they referred to **JOHN BOSA**, number one draft choice from Boston College, as Skybox Bosa: "That's what it took to sign him—a couple of skyboxes."

RICHARD BYRD, rookie lineman for the Houston Oilers, explaining why he joined a group of players who shaved their heads as a sign of solidarity: "I guess it was voluntary. There were ten other guys around me, so I volunteered."

Philadelphia Eagles coach **BUDDY RYAN**, on his relationship with owner **NORMAN BRAMAN**: "We're good friends now. I think he knows I'm doing a hell of a job. I've told him enough times."

In the late eighties, **MARIANNE JENNINGS** resigned as the faculty athletic representative at Arizona State when the university went over her head to restore the eligibility of linebacker **STACEY HARVEY**. "There are certain truths in life," Jennings told the Arizona *Republic*. "You don't spit into the wind, you don't tug on Superman's cape, and you don't mess with star football players."

JILL LEVY of Columbia, after the Lions set a major college record by losing their thirty-fifth consecutive football game: "We all like being at an academic institution where everyone is intellectual and no one can play football. I'm proud that our boys are wimps."

Said reserve running back **O.J. ANDERSON**, when asked his role with the N.Y. Giants" "My role? It's O.J., go over there. O.J., go back there. Now go over there, O.J. That's it. I have no role. I just do what they tell me."

Atlanta Falcons owner **RANKIN M. SMITH, SR.**, after cornerback **DEION SANDERS** arrived for a game in a limousine bigger than the one used by Smith: "That's all right. He has more money than I do."

Houston Oilers coach **JERRY GLANVILLE**, preparing for a Sunday game at Pittsburgh, said that he attended high school with Pirates manager **JIM LEYLAND** in Perrysburg, Ohio. "He would never come to school," Glanville said. "He'd make me skip school with him to play games. I can remember the principal bringing us to his office, and he said, 'You two will never be successful, you're always out there playing baseball and football. Neither one of you will end up worth a darn.' You know he might be right."

Denver coach **DAN REEVES** later joked about the thirty-five point knockout punch the Broncos took from the Washington Redskins in the second quarter of a Super Bowl game. "**MICHAEL SPINKS** makes all that money and after a first round knockout doesn't have to fight anymore that night. We had to stick around two more quarters."

From Grambling College football coach **EDDIE ROBINSON**, explaining why he hasn't had any drug problems with his players: "I have a meeting with them every year, and I explain to them that when you use drugs you lose your sex drive. You should see how big the eyes get."

From **GREG LOGAN** of *Newsday* on the New York Jets number one draft pick, **JEFF LAGEMAN** of Virginia: "If choice of courses at Virginia means anything, Lageman may have the aggressive tendencies the Jets are seeking. The title of his Anthropology class is 'Headhunting Rituals.'" Asked if he saw any analogy to football in the course, he replied, "Yeah, a lot."

How tough was football coach **VINCE LOMBARDI**? Said former Green Bay receiver **MAX McGEE**: "When he said sit down, I didn't even bother to look for a chair."

LOU HOLTZ, Notre Dame football coach: "The man who complains about the way the ball bounces is likely the one who dropped it."

Said Pittsburgh's **CRAG "IRONHEAD" HEYWARD** after being declared eligible for the NFL draft: "I'm just hoping to go in the first round. People are talking first round—or even higher."

Asked why wide receiver **CLARENCE VERDIN** of the Washington Redskins is called CNN, a teammate said, "Because he talks twenty-four hours a day."

Notre Dame football coach **LOU HOLTZ**: "I'm not a great motivator. I just get rid of guys who can't motivate themselves."

NFL football coach **BUDDY RYAN**, stressing leadership to his players, has this sign on his desk: "If you ain't the lead dog the scenery never changes."

ED GARVEY, former head of the National Football League Players Association, on former NFL Commissioner **PETE ROZELLE**: "Rozelle's been good for the legal profession—lawyers have made millions."

KATHY BOSWORTH, mother of tough linebacker **BRIAN BOSWORTH**, recalling some of his childhood shenanigans: "It's a good thing Brian was my third child, or he would have been the only one."

FRED GOLDSMITH, defensive coordinator at Arkansas, was named the new football coach at Rice. Why was he chosen to replace **JERRY BERNDT**? "Why we picked him over any particular individual, I don't know," said **J. EVANS ATTWELL**, chairman of the search committee.

PETER KING of *Newsday* reported that New York Giants football coach **BILL PARCELLS** had called a moratorium on dormitory pranks. **JIM BURT**, who leads the team in practical jokes, said: "Tell Bill that I don't know what moratorium means."

Said Miami Dolphins coach **DON SHULA** after a 27-0 loss to Buffalo: "The only thing we had today was **REGGIE ROY**'s punting, and anytime you have to talk about the punter as the highlight of the game, you're in deep trouble."

TV announcer **HARRY REASONER**, recalling an interview with Dallas Cowboys football coach **TOM LANDRY**, said he posed this question: "Coach, you are known as a conservative man with strict behavior codes for your players. But times have changed. For example, what if you had a halfback today who refused to get a haircut, who refused to wear a coat and tie, who smoked a joint every once in a while. How would you handle him?" According to Reasoner, Landry gave the question some thought before answering. Finally, he said, "How good a halfback?"

Said NBC's **CHARLIE JONES** when **ERIC DICKERSON** played for the Colts after the Los Angeles Rams had announced he was injured: "Dickerson has found a new miracle cure for thigh bruises. Just rub it with money."

Notre Dame football coach **LOU HOLTZ**, on the importance of time of possession: "The only important thing about the time of possession is who gets to keep the ball after the game is over."

From New England Patriots center **MIKE BABB**, who went to the University of Texas: "Back then I thought the most important thing was winning." And now? "Now it's winning and getting paid."

With its defensive line wiped out by injuries, the New York Jets flew in free agent **FRED DEAN** from San Diego and offered him $15,000 a game. Dean demanded $50,000 a game on a prorated basis. That was more than All-Star **MIKE GASTINEAU** was making. End of negotiations. "The only thing I can figure," Jets defensive lineman **BARRY BENNETT** told *Newsday*, "is that he had a friend in New York but didn't want to call long distance, so he flew across the country to make a local call."

LARRY FEISER of *The Sporting News*, on Tampa Bay coach **RAY PERKINS**: "On a personality scale of zero to ten, Perkins hovers around twenty-five below zero."

Said Notre Dame football coach **LOU HOLTZ**, after learning that *Sports Illustrated* might rank his team in the top twenty: "I told them the only way they could lose credibility quicker would be to put me in their swimsuit issue."

HANK BULLOUGH, head coach of the NFL Buffalo Bills, was establishing himself as the Yogi Berra of the NFL before the Bills fired him in 1986. Sample quotes:
"We'll have a good work ethnic."
"He did it on the spare of a moment."
"He's making improvement throwing the ball where he's throwing the ball."
"We keep beating ourselves, but we're getting better at it."
"It took the sails right out of our wind."
Of Bills' owner **RALPH WILSON**, he said, "I'm not a yes guy. He knows that when I hired him."

GARY BURBANK of Radio Station WLW in Cincinnati, on the new candy bar named for Bengals quarterback **BOOMER ESIASON**: "I think it comes in a sack."

***

When **BRIAN HOLLOWAY** was with the New England Patriots, he didn't endear himself to the Patriots front office after showing up at training camp with a water bed. Said *The Sporting News*: "One day there was a slow leak and the bed lost about twenty gallons of water. It created a mess, especially in the room below Holloway's, which happened to belong to Patriots general manger **PAT SULLIVAN**."

It was fun while it lasted but coach **BILL PARCELLS** would no longer get doused with Gatorade after victories by the N.Y. Giants. "Enough is enough," said designated dowser **HARRY CARSON**. "Maybe we'll do something different." Parcells' reply: "Good."

On CBS' "The NFL Today," **JIMMY "THE GREEK" SNYDER** called Denver's **JOHN ELWAY** far and away the best quarterback in the NFL. "Better than **DAN MARINO**?" **BRENT MUSBURGER** asked. "Better than anybody," Snyder said. Watching the show in his hotel room before taking the team bus to the Coliseum to face the Raiders was Elway himself. **BUDDY MARTIN** of the Denver *Post* asked him if he caught the Snyder segment. "Yeah, I heard it," he said. What did he think? Elway laughed. "I stood up and gave him a standing ovation," he said.

DUFFY DAUGGHERTY, when he was Michigan State football coach: "When you're playing for the national championship, it's not a matter of life or death. It's more important than that."

When a school teacher in Houston, Texas, told her fifth grade class to write a paper on the two greatest heroes in Texas' history, one student's entry was **JIM BOWIE** and **BUM PHILLIPS**. Bowie, of Alamo fame, seemed to be a logical choice but Phillips, head coach of the NFL's Houston Oilers? "Bum Phillips made a football fan out of Mother," the youngster said. "If he can do that, he has to be a hero."

Cincinnati Bengals offensive guard **MAX MONTOYA** explained why he is negotiating his own contract: "A lot of people have told me I'm crazy for not using an agent, but I think I know my situation better than any agent could. Besides," he added, "I'm cheaper."

University of Pittsburgh football coach **MIKE GOTTFRIED** recalls his debut as the Kansas University coach: "We were playing Northern Illinois. We had a great offense, but we couldn't stop them on defense. The score was 34–34 late in the game, and they tried a field goal and missed it, but we were offside. The penalty moved the ball forward and they tried again and made it. We lost 37–34. I'm running off the field and one of our fans leans out of the front row and yells, 'What are you going to do, Coach, when you play a really good team?' I felt bad for my players, having to listen to that loudmouth drunk, and then I recognized the voice of the president of the university."

Said Cleveland Browns nose tackle **BOB GOLIC**, when a columnist referred to him as a grizzled veteran: "Grizzled? I thought that was the tough part of a steak."

Kansas State football coach **STAN PARRISH** knew exactly what it sounded like when his team's chance for a thirty-eight yard field goal was blocked as time ran out against Kansas in the Futility Bowl and the game ended in a 17–17 tie. "I didn't watch it," said Parrish. "I heard it. It sounded like one of my four irons hitting a tree."

MIKE DITKA, when head coach of the Chicago Bears once remarked: "If I thought there was somebody else who could handle this job, let them handle it and I'll step aside." Chicago *Sun Times* columnist Terry Boers took him up on it, offering suggestions:
"Coach **STEVE GARVEY**—he could be the new Papa Bear."
"Coach **DEBORAH NORVILLE**—she's been replacing everyone else, so why not Ditka?"
"Coach **ZSA ZSA GABOR**—she knows a thing or two about the head slap."
"Coach **LEONA HELMSLEY**—mean, spiteful, and loves to treat people like dirt, so she'd fit right in."
"Coach **CURTIS STRANGE**—at least he knows how to win the Skins Game."

The Columbia University football team hadn't won a game in many a year but the Lions did end one streak. They took the lead in a game for the first time during one season. **KURT DASBACH** kicked a field goal to give the Lions a 10–7 lead over Lehigh. Was he excited? Slightly. "I completely forgot I had to kick off," he said.

Los Angeles *Times* alumnus **ED GILBERT**, adding to the list of malapropisms by announcers, submits a classic by veteran sports announcer **BILL STERN** during an Army-Navy game. As an Army player was being carried off the field, Stern said: "For his family and friends, he was not hurt, only injured, and is being helped to the sideline under his own power."

Said Oklahoma State coach **PAT JONES**, when asked the difference between his football material and that of next opponent, Oklahoma: "The pro scouts that come in here (to look over the team) can usually get their work done in one day. When they leave, I usually ask them where they're heading next. They'll say Oklahoma, and then say they'll probably be there three days."

ART SPANDER, in the San Francisco *Examiner*, referring to the football player problems at Florida State University: "And we used to think Florida State's biggest problem was field goal kicks that went wide right."

From Notre Dame coach **LOU HOLTZ**: "Somebody said to me, 'How can you call the plays from the sideline because you can't see anything?' and I said 'Well, that's the only place I ever watched a game from when I was playing.'"

In an attempt to display a light touch, **MIKE LYNN**, general manager of the Minnesota Vikings, showed up in the locker room wearing a Popeye hat. He served the players fried chicken, saying it was a substitute for spinach. "One of the things players have mentioned to me is that the only time they see me is when I'm disciplining them or negotiating a contract." Lynn said. "So I am going to be more visible when we're not in confrontation situations."

Before a game against South Carolina, Clemson coach **DANNY FORD** issued a gag order to his players, but defensive tackle **MICHAEL PERRY**, brother of **WILLIAM "REFRIGERATOR" PERRY**, said, "It doesn't bother me one way or the other, because I'm going to talk."

Notre Dame football coach **LOU HOLTZ** said that the man he admired most when he broke into coaching was **DARRELL ROYAL** at Texas University. "When I was an assistant coach at Connecticut," Holtz said, "I went to Austin (Texas) to see Royal. I was going to make the most of the time I had with him, and once I got into his office, I had a list of eighty questions I wanted to ask him. I knew he didn't expect this, and I'm certain he had to cancel a golf game because I took so much of his time. But he couldn't have been more gracious about helping me. I wrote down the answers to every one of those questions, and I still have them in a box somewhere. When you move as much as I do, you don't always unpack all the boxes."

Former great pro quarterback and then a CBS football analyst **KEN STABLER** after Detroit Lions quarterback **TODD HONS** had missed a wide open receiver in the end zone: "That'll get you back to selling cars in a hurry."

Michael Wilbon of The Washington *Post* reports on All Pro linebacker **CORNELIOUS BENNETT**: "He's a 235-pound linebacker who hits like **LAWRENCE TAYLOR** and runs like **CARL LEWIS**. He had 8.5 sacks in eight games as a rookie, including four in a season finale against the Philadelphia Eagles. One time he picked up quarterback **RANDALL CUNNINGHAM** after sacking him and said, "You'd better get somebody to block for you, or I'm going to kill you today."

The subject was puns, and Gus Schrader of the Cedar Rapids (Iowa) *Gazette* recalled that Tommy Fitzgerald of the Louisville *Courier-Journal* never passed up a chance to use one in his college football stories. In 1946, when Indiana upset Illinois 14–7, the winning score came after Illinois quarterback **PERRY MOSS** was sacked by a Hoosier end identified by Fitzgerald as **BILL STONE**. Here was Fitzgerald's lead in his reporting:

"Bloomington, Ind.—A rolling Stone gathers no Moss. Until final minutes of Saturday's superb football game here, that is, and then Indiana end Bill Stone rolled through Illinois blockers, knocked Perry Moss loose from the ball and recovered it in the end zone for a 14–7 victory."

After finishing his story, Fitzgerald joined the other writers at a tavern where he learned an alarming fact. A writer casually mentioned that the name of the Hoosier end who caused the fumble was **KAWALSKI**, not Stone. Fitzgerald was shocked. He rushed to the telephone to call his paper, asking them to change his story. The paper was right on deadline, but the deskman said that he'd do the best he could. The next morning, Fitzgerald picked up the paper and was horrified to see this lead:

"Bloomington, Ind.—A rolling Kawalski gathers no Moss. Until the final minutes..."

Chicago Bear coach **MIKE DITKA** on quarterback **JIM McMAHON'S** off- season surgery: "The shoulder surgery was a success. The lobotomy failed."

Quarterback **RANDALL CUNNINGHAM** of the Philadelphia Eagles, asked if he made a ninety-five cent telephone call to vote for himself after he was nominated for making one of the best passes on "Monday Night Football": "No, it cost too much money."

RAGHIB ISMAIL, the speedy Notre Dame pass catcher who caught a fifty-five yard pass from quarterback TONY RICE in an Irish victory over the University of Southern California, was the Pennsylvania high school sprint champion. He's nicknamed The Rocket. His mother, interviewed on television during the Notre Dame-Penn State game, said that she has two other sons who are nicknamed The Missile and The Bomb. "And they call me The Launch Pad," she said.

Cleveland Browns coach MARTY SCHOTTENHEIMER had a 35–28 record after succeeding SAM RUTIGLIANO, who was a favorite of the sports writers because of his quick wit. Schottenheimer was a bit different. During the National Football League players' strike, he was asked if the strike situation was bizarre. The English major in him answered: "To say something is bizarre is to say it is outside of reality. This situation definitely is realty. These games count."

Pro football's SID GILLMAN, asked to name the greatest quarterback he's ever seen, told Greg Logan of *Newsday*: "JOE NAMATH was probably the best, but every time I look at DAN MARINO, I think, 'My god, is it physically possible to get rid of the football any faster.'" Gillman said that it usually takes three or four years for a quarterback to develop but said of Marino, "He's the seven-year-old violin prodigy who makes his debut with the Philharmonic." Some coaches believe the role of the quarterback is overemphasized, but Gillman said, "You don't know how important a quarterback is until you don't have one."

Oklahoma football coach BARRY SWITZER, on taking his team to Miami for participation in the annual Orange Bowl for the ninth time: "At least I won't need a tour guide."

From RICHARD DENT of the Chicago Bears, comparing defensive coach VINCE TOBIN with his predecessor, BUDDY RYAN: "Buddy is definitely a better coach than Vince because he's been in the business longer. Vince is a good coach, too, don't get me wrong." (Open mouth, insert cleat?)

When the Fordham University football team used to play at home on Saturday afternoons, the pregame meal usually consisted of bacon and eggs. Once, on a Friday night, the Rams had a game at Iona College, a short bus trip. "We called the dining service and said we're going to eat at 3:30 P.M. and the game is at 7:30 P.M.," Coach **LARRY GLUECK** said. "We didn't even think about telling them what to fix for us. We got what they were going to serve to the regular students on Friday night—Mexican food. As a coach, I've always said, 'I want to see fire in your eyes.' I don't think we had fire in our eyes, but we sure had fire in our stomachs." The fired-up Rams won 31–29.

If they give a hyperbole-of-the-year award, one of the leaders in the clubhouse would have to be San Francisco 49ers tackle **HARRIS BARTON**, who told the San Jose *Mercury News*: "When a player like **RANDY CROSS** (outstanding lineman for the 49ers) goes down, it's like losing **JOE DIMAGGIO**."

MARTY SCHOTTENHEIMER, then coach of the Cleveland Browns, wasn't quite sure which was worse—**FRANK MINNIFIELD'S** play or the player's explanation. Minnifield, after intercepting a pass against the Houston Oilers, scrambled around looking for running room, and when he couldn't find any, he flung a wild lateral that sailed over the head of fellow defensive back **HANFORD DIXON**, who wasn't looking for a lateral. The ball flew out of bounds. Said Schottnheimer: "That's the kind of stuff you do when you're six years old and playing in the backyard. After the game, I told Frank to remember that the ball is valuable. You should have heard his logic. He said, 'Coach, did you see Hanford? I'm running and Hanford won't block anybody. So I figure, I'm gonna give Hanford the ball and let them tackle Hanford.'"

Chicago Bear great defensive tackle **STEVE McMICHAEL**, when discussing the fine Philadelphia Eagles quarterback **RANDALL CUNNINGHAM**: "I'd go so far as to say he's the best athlete in NFL history to play that position. I'd much rather play against an old guy like **JOE MONTANA**. He goes down when you breathe on him."

The Atlanta Falcons' media guide, explaining why coach **MARION CAMPBELL** is called Swamp Fox, says that his full name is Francis Marion Campbell, Jr. And that he's named for the Revolutionary War hero Francis Marion who was famous for fighting in the swamps of Campbell's native South Carolina. Good story but it's not the one Campbell told the St. Petersburg *Times*. He said: "When I was playing at the University of Georgia, the publicist asked me if I was named after Francis Marion, the Swamp Fox. I said 'No,' and he said, 'When you look in the paper tomorrow, you will be.'"

Tom Yantz of the Hartford *Courant* reports that the U.S. Coast Guard Academy, rated the most selective college in America by USA Today, accepts about 9 percent of its applicants. The SAT average for freshmen at the Academy is 1200, according to its admissions office. Yantz quotes **PETE MINGO**, a starting offensive tackle in the Division III football team; "You can't watch 'Cheers' and make it here."

It was okay when **ED "TOO TALL" JONES** made opposing quarterbacks hear bells, but the Dallas Cowboys didn't like it when bells went off in the dressing room. So they asked the veteran defensive lineman to take a powder—elsewhere. Cowboys officials had been mystified for several years about the fire alarm system at the practice facility at Valley Ranch in Irving, Texas. The system would go off time and time again, apparently for no good reason. But a thorough investigation pegged Jones as the culprit, said the Fort Worth *Star-Telegram*. The problem? He's living up to his nickname—he's just too tall. One of the facility's smoke detectors in located above Too Tall's locker. And on some occasions when the 6' 9" lineman has sprinkled talcum powder over his body following a post-practice shower, he is tall enough that the flying powder has set off the fire alarm system. After the Cowboys asked him to apply powder away from the area, there was a marked drop in the number of false alarms. "We're either going to have to get shorter linemen or less sensitive fire alarms," said **DOUG TODD**, Cowboys' public relations director.

A mind-boggling thought. Among the newer rules passed by National Football League owners was one that included a provision forbidding a drop-kick beyond the line of scrimmage. Can anyone remember seeing a drop-kick, from anywhere, in the NFL in the past fifty years?

Notre Dame coach **LOU HOLTZ**, on the length of the grass at the Air Force Academy's Falcon Field in Colorado Springs, Colorado: "If my front yard was like that, my wife would have a fit."

GIL BRANDT, Dallas Cowboys vice-president, on the use of computers in the NFL annual player draft: "I'll say one thing for computers. They never try to sell you their brother-in-law as a prospect."

GARY SHELTON of the St. Petersburg (Florida) *Times* wrote that there were two reasons the New York Giants football team wanted running back **HERSCHEL WALKER**: "One, they could use him to replace **DAVE MEGGETT**" (who had left the Giants to sign with the New England Patriots). "Two, if it doesn't work out, they can trade Herschel to the Minnesota Vikings for six starters and thirty-two draft picks."

Having played on the losing team in four straight Super Bowls, **JIM KELLY**, Buffalo Bills quarterback, felt revenge was never out of his mind. Kelly was one of the celebrity guests in attendance at a charity auction of sports memorabilia in Charleston, South Carolina, when an autographed photo of Dallas cowboys owner **JERRY JONES** and coach **JIMMY JOHNSTON** was placed on auction. Kelly, the quarterback whose Bills lost to the Cowboys in the last two Super Bowls, quickly sprang into the bidding action. After claiming the picture for the top bid of $500, he promptly tore it into little pieces. Said Kelly, "It was worth every penny."

Owner **ART MODELL** of the National Football League's Cleveland Browns: "**VINCE LOMBARDI** wrote the book on coaching, **DON SHULA** edited it."

Arizona Cardinal head coach **BUDDY RYAN** recently purchased a piece of the contract of middleweight boxer **FRANKIE RHODES**. "His right hand is much better than mine," Ryan said, alluding to the punch he threw at fellow Houston Oiler assistant coach **KEVIN GILBRIDE** during a game in 1993.

JACK LAMBERT, former Pittsburgh Steeler All-Star linebacker, on quarterback **CRAIG MORTON**: "I kind of like Craig Morton. I think he's an overachiever. The reason I like him, though, is because he couldn't run out of the pocket."

DEWEY SELMAN, Tampa Bay Buccaneer linebacker, who is working on a Ph.D. in Philosophy at Oklahoma: "Philosophy is just a hobby. You can't open up a philosophy factory."

TONY "MACK THE SACK" McGEE, New England Patriot defensive end, describing how he felt after failing to have any sacks in a game against the Miami Dolphins: "Angry. Disappointed. Mad. Sad. Disgusted, busted, and can't be trusted."

VERNON HOLLAND, Cincinnati Bengal tackle, recounting a dream in which he had been traded: "I don't know who got me. I dream in black and white, so I couldn't tell what color the uniforms were."

ROCKY BLIER, Pittsburgh Steeler running back, marveling at coach Chuck Noll's self-confidence: "He's the only person I know who ever bought an airplane before he learned to fly."

GARY YEPREMIAN, New Orleans Saint kicker, after deciding against a $10,000 hair implant: "The thing that really bothers me is that there are already so many Elvis Presley look-alikes."

DAN PASTORINI, Houston Oilers quarterback, on what it's like to hand off the ball to running back **ERIC CAMPBELL**: "Comforting."

DAVE GRAF, Cleveland Brown linebacker, on an ovation afforded teammate **DINO HALL**, who is 5'7": "When the crowd started chanting, 'Dino, Dino,' his parents must have felt five feet tall."

BUM PHILLIPS, Houston Oilers coach, assessing the talents of running back **EARL CAMPBELL**: "Earl may not be in a class by himself, but whatever class he's in, it doesn't take long to call the roll."

ERNIE HOLMES, former Pittsburgh Steeler tackle, explaining his decision to embark on a professional boxing career: "When **MUHAMMAD ALI** put down his gloves and picked up his fork, I put down my fork and picked up my gloves."

GORDON BEARD, Associated Press sports editor in Baltimore, on the proliferation of NFL playoff teams: "If **PETE ROZELLE** had been in charge of the league during World War II, Germany and Japan would still be in the running, and Ethiopia would have been a wild-card finalist."

JOHN MACKEY, former Baltimore Colt tight end, lamenting the absence of a black head coach in the National Football League: "I look at all the coaches in the game today and I think to myself there's no reason why a black coach can't lose too."

SAM RUTIGLIANO, Cleveland Browns coach, on how to stop Seattle's scrambling quarterback, **JIM ZORN**: "Well, you could give your outside linebackers hand grenades."

JOHNNY WALKER, disc jockey at Baltimore's radio station WSBR: "The University of Maryland football team members all make straight A's. Their B's are a little crooked."

TOM BASS, Tampa Bay Buccaneer defensive coordinator and author of two volumes of poetry: "If I had to work twenty hours a day and sleep on a cot in my office, I'd chalk it all up. Some of my best defensive ideas come when I'm looking at sunsets."

RON MEYERS, Southern Methodist coach, on Rice's 6' 8" tight end, **ROBERT HUBBLE**: "When he's covered, he's open."

WEBB ENBANK, former New York Met coach, asked to assess **JOE NAMATH'S** performance in a stage production of "Picnic": "I'll have to wait until I see the films."

BUM PHILLIPS, Houston Oiler coach: "**EARL CAMPBELL** ain't like those high priced, spoiled athletes. Why he had me over to his office the other day just like one of the guys."

PETE ROZELLE, marveling at how little controversy NFL officials had stirred up during the season: "They might be waiting for the playoffs."

TOM MASON, Arizona football coach, on the difficulty of recruiting against Southern California coach **JOHN ROBINSON**: "I sell cactus. He sells Heismans."

CARL MAUCK, Houston Oiler center, hearing the news that one of the team's lineman will receive a twenty-five pound assortment of steaks and sausages after every game in which **EARL CAMPBELL** rushes for 100 years next season: "Can they work out something to get us some gas?"

HATTIE WALKER, about the possibility that her grandson, Notre Dame's **VEGAS FERGUSON**, who she raised, might win the Heisman Trophy: "I don't have room for it. It'd just be something I'd have to dust."

CARL PARSLEY, Houston Oiler punter, on kicking specialists' salaries: "People think our income is much greater than it really is. I'm barely making enough to pay off my Cadillac."

TERRY BRADSHAW, Pittsburgh Steeler quarterback, after nine turnovers helped Cincinnati upset the Steelers 34–10: "I just know the dog's going to bite me when I get home."

JACK ELWAY, San Jose State football coach, on the effect that college life is having on his son **JOHN**, who is starring as quarterback at Stanford as a freshman: "I really don't see that many changes in him so far. Hell, he never did take out the garbage."

ED FARRELL, Davidson football coach, after losing to Furman 63–55: "I thought fifty-five would have been enough."

DON SHULA, Miami Dolphins' Hall of Fame football coach, had just won back-to-back Super Bowls, making him one of the most recognized faces in America while losing his privacy at the same time. So Shula decided to go someplace where he had a chance to be anonymous and have a vacation with his wife and kids. He chose Maine. "We decided to go to the movies one night in this little town," recalled Shula. "When we walked into the show, all the lights were on and there were six or seven people sitting around. Suddenly they all got up and started to applaud. I couldn't believe it. I said to the nearest guy, 'How did you recognize me?' He said, 'Buddy, I don't know who the hell you are. We clapped because we needed three more people before they'd start the movie.'"

After being bitten by a snake, coach **JERRY GLANVILLE** of the Houston Oilers had to sign a waiver before a doctor would allow him to be on the sidelines before a game. Glanville said that the doctor told him: "I really don't care if you die. I just don't want to lose my license."

Said NBC pro football commentator **PAUL McGUIRE**: "It's just a game. It's nothing monumental. These guys are making a million dollars a year to play a kid's game. If that's not fun, I don't know what is."

Former San Diego Chargers kicker and then-"Wheel of Fortune" host **ROLF BENIRSCHKE**: "If I ever do marry and have kids and one day my grandchildren ask me what I've done for a living, I'm going to feel a little funny when I try to explain what I did for a living. For ten years I kicked around a crazy football, then I spend the rest of my time asking people if they want to buy a vowel."

Green Bay Packer assistant coach **DICK MODZELEWDSI**, after head coach **FORREST GREGG** had left to take the head coaching job at Southern Methodist: "The recruiting there is not like the pro draft. You have to kiss people. I can't see Forrest kissing Mom and Pop to get their kid to go to SMU."

ED CROOKE, New York Giants publicist, on the weight problems of 295-pound defensive end **LEONARD MARSHALL**: "We put him on a Cambridge diet and he ate half of Cambridge."

PART 4

BOXING

A Brief History

Boxing, often referred to as "the manly art of self-defense," is a sport in which two competitors try to hit each other with fists encased in gloves while attempting to avoid each other's blows. The fight is divided into a specified number of rounds, three minutes long, with one minute rest periods between rounds.

Amateur boxing matches consist of three to five rounds. The recognized length of championship fights is twelve rounds. In all boxing, winners are determined either by a decision of the judges (who keep points or round victors on a score card as the fight progresses), the referee, or both. The winner also may be decided by a knockout, in which one rival is knocked to the floor by a punch and is unable to get up within ten seconds. A doctor or the referee can declare the boxer injured or defenseless even if there is no knockdown. A tied or even match is ruled a draw.

A boxing ring is actually a square twelve to twenty feet on each side and enclosed on each side by three or four ropes. Since 1892, gloves have been worn by boxers. These gloves are made of leather, have no finger holes except for the thumb, and weigh from eight ounces for amateur fights to six ounces for professional and all title fights.

Because of its violent nature and its identification with betting, boxing has had a controversial history. In 1866, the marquees of Queensberry gave his support to a new set of rules which limited the number of three minute rounds, eliminated gouging and wrestling, and made the use of gloves mandatory.

BOXING

Boxer **GEORGE FOREMAN:** "I'd like to get a steamroller and lay (All-Pro defensive lineman) **KEN NORTON** down and crush him flat. Other than that, I like him."

JOHN TATE, heavyweight boxer: "Any fighter who tries to psyche me out is wasting his time, because I know what's in his mind. I don't fear anybody but God. Another boxer might knock you down, but God can do something permanent to you."

HUGH MALEY, FNN-SCORE boxing announcer, on **GEORGE FOREMAN**: "Some fighters telegraph their punches. Ol'George has resorted to carrier pigeons."

Boxer **GEORGE FOREMAN** didn't think boxer **MIKE TYSON** would have much trouble defeating **MICHAEL SPINKS**, but said Tyson was overmatched against (wife) **ROBIN GIVENS**. "In time she'll get him," said Foreman of Tyson's wife. "You can be dethroned in your own home. A woman can bring you to your knees. Tyson thinks he's 5-foot-11, but she can make him 2-foot-11." Tyson might disagree, but he can't deny that Foreman speaks from experience. George has been married five times.

Heavyweight champion **MIKE TYSON**, after challenger **TYRELL BIGGS** told reporters that he has a plan for beating Tyson: "Everybody has plans until they get hit the first time."

Boxer **WILLIE PASTRANO**, to a ring doctor who asked if he knew where he was after being knocked down by Jose Torres in a lightweight title bout: "You're damn right I know where I am. I'm in Madison Square Garden getting beat up."

Boxer **GEORGE FOREMAN**, to reporters after his victory over **ALEX STEWART**, a bout that left Foreman with a broken nose, two swollen eyes, and a swollen jaw:; "Ask me how I feel and you're going to get it."

JOE FRAZIER, former heavyweight boxing champion: "You can map out a fight plan or a life plan, but when the action starts, it may not go the way you planned, and you're down to your reflexes— which means your training. That's where your road work shows. If you cheated on that in the dark of the mornin', well, you're gettin' found out now under the bright lights."

Former heavyweight champion **GEORGE FOREMAN,** on his seven straight comeback victories: "It's great being a celebrity again. I go home and my wife doesn't make me take out the garbage. I don't even have to pick up my clothes either."

LARRY HOLMES, scheduled to fight **MIKE TYSON,** claimed Tyson fought dirty against **TYRELL BIGGS:** "If he tries any of that stuff with me, the head butts and the elbows, I'll do it right back. It'll be like Hulk Hogan versus the Junkyard Dog."

From former heavyweight champion **LARRY HOLMES,** on **MIKE TYSON'S** decision to drop manager **BILL CLAYTON** and join forces with promoter **DON KING,** Holmes' former nemesis: "You don't get off the horse that brought you over the bridge, to get on another horse, especially not that horse. I know that horse too well."

SUGAR RAY LEONARD, former boxing great, announced that as a manager he will spar with his fighters: "I'll get in the ring and work with all of them. They know my reputation, and that they'll have to concentrate while sparring with me. There's nothing like a stiff punch to make you listen."

Boxing promoter **DON KING,** on his relationship with boxer **JULIO CESAR CHAVEZ:** "We have a marriage—like a father and a son."

JAMES "QUICK" TILLIS tells of his first trip to Chicago to launch his boxing career: "I put down my suitcase and looked up at the Sears Tower and said, 'Chicago, I'm going to conquer you.' When I looked down my suitcase was gone."

Boxer **MIKE TYSON'S** record was 33–0. **MICHAEL SPINKS,** his scheduled opponent, was 32–0. Said promoter **BUTCH LEWIS:** "Somebody's zero has to go."

Former light-heavyweight boxing champ **ARCHIE MOORE,** on his new diet: "You can eat anything you want as long as you don't swallow it."

IRVING RUDD, boxing publicist, on the ego of boxer **HEC-TOR CAMACHO,** who calls himself the Macho Man: "Hector Camacho's great dream is to someday die in his own arms."

Here's a quote and guess who said it: "I feel sorry for those fighters who have to come back for one more shot. Eventually they get their jaws rattled and they're walking on their heels. They're an embarrassment to their families, to themselves, and to boxing." (**GEORGE FOREMAN**, April 1980.)

Before making his boxing comeback, **GEORGE FOREMAN'S** weight had climbed to 312 pounds. "I went to a basketball game one night and some people hollered at me," he said. "I thought they knew me. Not so. They thought I was '**REFRIGERATOR' PERRY.**"

When referee **VICTOR DRAKULICH** separated junior middleweights **JULIO CAESAR GREEN** and **LONNY BEASLEY** during the twelfth round of a closely contested fight in Las Vegas, he apparently punched Beasley a little too hard. Beasley fell flat on his back, didn't get up, and was counted out by Drakulich, who was chased out of the ring by one of Beasley's angry cornermen. Said Drakulich: "If they're not able to remain standing when you break them up, they shouldn't be allowed to fight."

IRVING RUDD, Top Rank publicist, on working at the training camp of boxer **THOMAS HEARNS**: "Hearns and I had a very close relationship. There's nothing I wouldn't do for him, and there's nothing he wouldn't do for me. And that's how it's been for ten years now—we've done nothing for each other."

GEORGE FOREMAN, forty years old and weighing 250 pounds, said after his thirteenth consecutive knockout since leaving retirement in March 1987: "I'm a better fighter now than I have ever been. I could have lost weight, but I started thinking, 'Why would a lion lose weight to fight a house cat?' If you're a bigger guy, you hit harder."

When told that **TONY MANDARICH**, a 300-pound Green Bay Packers draftee, was being ballyhooed as an opponent for **MIKE TYSON**, former New York Jets star **JOE KLECKO**, who boxed at Temple, recalled an afternoon with former heavyweight champion **JOE FRAZIER**: "I'd never sparred with Frazier before, but now I was in there banging with him and I guess I got a little too loose," Klecko told the New York *Times*. "He threw a left hook, but he stopped it right there next to my head, then he laughed. That one left hook was enough for me to realize that I didn't really want to be a boxer."

Boxing great **MUHAMMAD ALI**, explaining how he wants to be remembered: "That he took a few cups of love and one teaspoon of patience. One tablespoon of generosity. One pint of kindness. One quart of laughter, mixed it all up, and stirred it well. And then he spread it over the span of a lifetime and served it to each and every deserving person he met."

GEORGE CHUVALO, forty-one, who was stripped of the Canadian heavyweight championship he held for twenty-one years, after a dispute with that country's boxing official: "I am the best heavyweight fighter in Canada, and I'll be the best until I'm dead seven years."

Heavyweight champion **MUHAMMAD ALI**, to a seatmate during a turbulent flight from Atlanta to Los Angeles: "This isn't going to crash. I'm on it."

Boxer **TRACY STEELE**, who has lost six of nine pro fights but isn't about to hang up the gloves: "I have the heart of a racehorse trapped inside the body of a jackass."

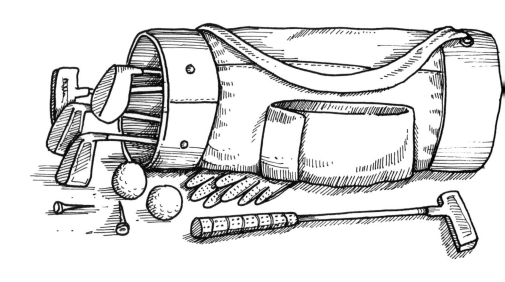

PART 5

GOLF

A Brief History

Golf is a sport in which a player uses a long shafted club to propel a small, hard ball around a large area of land, having a number of widely spaced holes. The object is to put the ball into the holes, in order, using the least possible number of shots. The game may be played by two or more individual opponents or by opposing teams.

A golf course covers from fifty to one hundred fifty acres of ground, preferably on rolling terrain. The course is a large grassed area, with obstacles (tall grass, trees, and bushes) throughout. The course is divided into a series of holes, each representing a unit of competition in itself. A game, or round, of golf consists of eighteen holes.

Each hole on the course has a teeing ground or starting place; a green or section that contains the target (a hole in the ground called a cup); a fairway from the teeing ground to the green; and the rough is natural and prepared obstacles in or near the route to the green. Tees and greens are numbered and holes must be played in sequence—that is, from the first tee to the first green, second tee to second green, and so on, until the round is completed on the eighteenth hole.

The Scots are credited with originating the modern game of golf. Its popularity in Scotland in the mid-fifteenth century was such that King James II prevailed on Parliament to de-emphasize the game so that people would devote more attention to archery, a sport important to the defense of the country.

GOLF

Said **JERRY PATE**, ESPN golf analyst, as **NICK FALDO** addressed a four-foot putt to save par in the British Open: "You're not going to see him miss many of these." Faldo then missed the putt for a bogey.

Golfer **LEE TREVINO**, on meeting Prime Minister Edward Heath in 1978: "How do you do, Mr. Prime Minister. Ever shake hands with a Mexican before?"

BIRCH RIBER, chairman of the LPGA Tournament in Mason, Ohio, where **NANCY LOPEZ** and her husband have bought a condominium near one owned by baseball pitching great **TOM SEAVER** and his wife: "Nancy's probably a drive and a five-iron from the Seavers. For anyone else it would be a drive and two three-irons."

Hall of Fame golfer **BEN HOGAN**: "I dreamed one time—and this sounds crazy—that I made seventeen holes-in-one, and on the eighteenth hole, I lipped the cup, and I was just madder than hell."

Anonymous quote about the well-publicized divorce proceedings between golfer **FRED COUPLES** and wife **DEBORAH**, who requested money to support her polo ponies: "In any divorce, it's the polo ponies that suffer most."

When **GARY PLAYER** suggested that his two wins in the U.S. Senior Open be counted as major championships, **JACK NICKLAUS** said, "Oh, you know Gary. If he wins the Bangkok Four Ball, he thinks it should be counted as a major."

Golf great **TOM WATSON**, on how he helped the golf game of former President **GERALD FORD**: "First, hitting the ball. Second, finding out where it went."

Orlando *Sentinel* columnist **LARRY GUEST**, on the views of pro golfer **MAC O'GRADY**: "One camp thinks he's a genius who can really play golf; the other side is equally certain he's a crackpot who can really play."

Pro golfer **PAUL AZINGER** was disqualified from the Doral Open Tournament after a TV viewer called to inform tour officials that he broke a rule by accidentally moving a pebble with his hand in a hazard. A day after the incident occurred, it didn't sit well with fellow pro **JOHN MAHAFFEY**, who said, "It would be like calling up after a Super Bowl game and saying, look, there was holding on that touchdown in the fourth quarter, so we'll have to take the touchdown away from you and you're going to lose the game."

PATTY SHEEHAN, LPGA tour great: "I like the idea of playing for money. I never did like to polish silverware."

Pro Golfer **SEVE BALLESTEROS**, asked if he and **LEE TREVINO** conversed in Spanish during a practice round: "No, Trevino speaks Mexican."

JACK NICKLAUS and North Carolina basketball coach **DEAN SMITH** teamed up in an exhibition of golf match against a pair of collegians on a course Nicklaus designed in Banner Elk, North Carolina. After a shaky start, Nicklaus and Smith moved to one up after five holes. At that point, Nicklaus turned to Smith and said, "Now that we've got the lead, do we go into four corners?"

When golfer **HOWARD TWITTY**, who stands 6'5" and weighs 210 pounds, was asked why he never played football, he said: "Because I always felt I'd like to keep all my blood inside my body."

Rice University golf coach **JOHN PLUMBLEY**, after a particularly bad practice day by the Rice team in which squirrels, birds, and other animals were threatened and forced to scatter when his players went to the tee: "We've set back the mating season in Texas by ninety days."

Golfer **LEE TREVINO**: "There are no rich Mexicans. They get some money and they call themselves Spanish."

Said **GREG NORMAN**, after a fan told him he had lost a bet on him in a PGA tournament: "Sorry, mate, but don't feel too bad. I didn't make any money here either."

At the British Open, **SANDY LYLE** was seen wearing a button that said, "It's not whether you win or lose—but whether I do."

CHI CHI RODRIGUEZ, lamenting the fact he weighs only 132 pounds. "If I could drive the ball just twenty years further I could beat anybody in the world. I have to swing hard, I'm so small. I got my start in golf as ball marker, you know."

A young woman in an expensive car pulled into a parking spot in a shopping mall in Seattle and stepped inside. Her vanity license plate read "Hole in One." When she returned to her car, a motorist shouted to her, "What's your handicap?" She instinctively replied, "About thirteen" but wondered why he asked. Then, as she drove away, she noted the sign: "Handicap Parking Only."

Senior PGA Tour golfer **BOB BRUE** recalls playing with an amateur who was so used to cheating on every hole that when he made a hole-in-one, he wrote down "0" on his card.

From senior golfer **GARY PLAYER**, recalling his early days on the tour: "I would travel with my wife, five kids, a nurse, thirty-three suitcases, reserve three hotel rooms, and take three taxis. I had to win just to break even."

From **LANNY WADKINS**, who planned to play in the pro golfers Hawaiian Open: "After Hawaii I'm taking a week off at Mauna Lani (to fulfill a contract obligation). Lie on the beach. Work on my tan. Have a beverage. It's a tough job, but somebody has to do it."

Golfer **JOSE-MARIA OLAZBAL** of Spain, resisting suggestions he change putters during a slump on the greens: "It's not the arrow, it's the Indian."

PGA Seniors Tour golfer **CHI CHI RODRIGUEZ** on his go-for-broke style of playing golf: "If they put the queens flag on the *Titanic*, I'll go for it."

PGA Tour regular **GEORGE ARCHER**: "If it wasn't for golf, I'd probably be a caddie today."

Said Scotland's **SANDY LYLE** when asked the difference between the British Open, which he won in 1985, and the Tournament Players Championship he was entering: "About 120 years."

MAC O'GRADY, after a practice round for the U.S. Open in San Francisco, had this to say about the course, with its sloping fairways and undulating greens: "The inclinations and topography of the Olympic Club course already disturb the vesicular semicircular canals of my inner ear balancing centers."

TED WILLIAMS, Boston Red Sox slugger, rated by many as baseball's greatest hitter, once needled **SAM SNEAD**, one of the all-time great golfers: "Look," said Williams, "you use a club with a flat hitting surface and belt a stationary object. What's so tough about that? I gotta stand up there with a round bat and hit a ball that is traveling at me 110 miles an hour—and curving." Snead responded: "Yeah, Ted, but you don't have to go up in the stands and play all your foul balls."

JACK NICKLAUS, on his golf game: "I got contact lenses so I could see. Now I can see, and I can't make anything."

Asked what he would do with his winnings after winning the 1968 U.S. Open, golfer **LEE TREVINO** said, "I may buy the Alamo and give it back to Mexico."

LEE TREVINO on his anticipation, years ago, for playing on the Senior Tour: "I can't wait. I'm fifty in December. Hell, if I could find my birth certificate, I might be fifty already."

CHI CHI RODRIGUEZ, senior golfer, to a partner who had landed an approach shot below a steep ridge: "If you dig deep enough there, you might find **JIMMY HOFFA**."

When **PAUL AZINGER** temporarily withdrew from the golf tour to begin treatments for cancer, one of the calls that touched him the most came from golf great **JOHNNY MILLER**. Said Azinger: "He told me, 'Zinger, it's not what we accomplish in life that matters, it's what we overcome. You have to overcome something far greater than what most people have to overcome. That's the reality you're facing.'"

BOB HOPE, on how to find former President **GERALD FORD** on the golf course: "Just follow the wounded."

European Ryder Cup golf team captain **BERNARD GAL-LACHER**, when asked the name of the team's doctor: "I don't know. We all call him Doc."

The newest thing on the PGA's Senior Tour was the Centinela training center, a mobile fitness facility. "Hey, even **BILLY CASPER** is in there riding the bicycle," said **GAY BREWER**. "Of course he took a golf cart to get there."

NICK FALDO, great English golfer, after narrowly missing some crucial putts in a Ryder Cup four-ball match: "All we need to do is get back into the team room, hit our heads against the wall a few times, and we'll all be okay.

Golfer **LEE TREVINO**, after turning fifty and joining the Senior Tour: "For the first time in a long time, I'll be playing against people my own age."

JACK STEVENS, long one of the most influential men in the South, became the fourth chairman in the history of the Augusta National Golf Club. Stephens, the chief architect of Stephens, Inc., the country's largest investment bank outside of Wall Street, had taken over the leadership of Augusta National with organized softness and deftness that bodes well for the future of this prestigious golf club. According to club lore, Stephens was once paired in a foursome with a guest of another member, who mocked Stephens for suggesting they play for $2 Nassau. "I normally play a $100 Nassau," said the guest. After the round, when the foursome sat down to a gin game for Stephen's usual stakes of a penny a point, the guest was even more disdainful. Finally annoyed Stephens calmly asked the man his net worth. "Twelve and a half million," the guest said. "Fine," Stephens is reputed to have answered. "I'll match that, and we'll cut the cards for it." When the guest was rendered speechless, Stephens' soft voice intoned: "Penny a point then," he said.

Said ESPN analyst **BRUCE DEVLIN** as **MAC O'GRADY** teed off on the par-three fifteenth in the PGA: "A lot of people have a lot of respect for this man's golf swing." So did the gallery. His shot had them running for cover.

Senior Golfer **CHI CHI RODRIGUEZ**, defending his diet, which is heavy on meat: "Have you ever seen a bad-looking lion or tiger?"

Senior Golfer **CHI CHI RODRIGUEZ**, Puerto Rico's gift to the Senior Pro Golf Tour, discussing his Latin American accent: "It's embarrassing at times. The other day I asked my caddie for my sand wedge, and ten minutes later he came back with a ham on rye."

When **BILL RUSSELL** returned to coaching with the Sacramento Kings, old friend **K.C. JONES** was surprised. He didn't think his old roommate would ever again take a job that would cut into his golf game. "He'd play seven days a week, thirty-six holes a day if he could," Jones said. "He's a maniac. He lives in Seattle, and if he wants to go out and play and it's raining, he'll get on a plane and fly down to California and play there." Russell once said, "When I was growing up, my mother wouldn't allow me to go near a golf course. She didn't think the people who played were very nice. Now I play every day, and you know what? She was right."

By the nature of the sport, golf stories are not only plentiful but are usually smugly humorous. One such story concerns a golfer who, after driving the ball off the tee into the rough, pretended he was looking for the ball but was mainly concerned with stomping down on the grass around it. Looking somewhat confused as he peered at the distant green, he asked his caddie if he could possibly reach the green with a three-wood. "Nope," said the caddie. "It takes about three or four more stomps for a three-wood."

Said **CHI CHI RODRIGUEZ**, when asked by ESPN when he realized he was a good golfer: "When I played nine holes with **JACK NACKLAUS** and won two of them."

In his golf book, **BOB HOPE** tells about an old-timer who could hit the ball pretty well but couldn't see where it went. Consequently he had a hard time getting a game. One day the pro told him: "Charlie, I've got just the right partner for you. Tom's about your age and he's got eyes like a hawk." So a few days later the two oldsters got together. On the first tee, Charlie hit his driver, turned to Tom, and anxiously asked, "Did you see it?" Tom replied, "Yep!" Charlie: "Where did it go?" After a slight pause, Tom said: "Gee, I forgot."

PART 6

ICE HOCKEY

A Brief History

Ice hockey is played on an ice surface, or rink, and each team features six players. Each player has a bladed stick that he uses to advance a hard rubber disk called a puck. The object is to hit the puck into a netted cage and score a goal, the winner being the team scoring the most goals at the end of the game. Each team consists of three players on a forward's line (right and left wingmen and a center), a right and left defense man, and a goaltender. The game is played in three twenty-minute periods, with a ten-minute intermission between periods.

A regulation rink is 200 feet long and 85 feet wide with rounded corners of a 15-foot radius. The entire surface is enclosed with four-foot-high wooden boards. Posts for a goal cage in the center of each goal line are four feet high and six feet apart; they are connected at the top by a horizontal bar. The posts, crossbar, and arcs are attached to netting that extends back at least seventeen inches from the top and down to the ice. In front of the cage is a four-feet deep by eight-feet wide rectangular area, called the "crease." This is the goaltender's domain, where he has certain privileges that the other players do not. No opposing player can stay in or score from the "crease."

Some of the greatest hockey names include Maurice Richard, Bobby Hill, Gordie Howe, Bobby Orr, and Wayne Gretzky.

ICE HOCKEY

JIM CRAIG, outstanding U.S.A. hockey goalie, after an inter-section near Boston University was renamed "Olympic Four Place" in honor of himself and three other alumni who played on the Olympic hockey team: "Do I still have to pay the $500 worth of parking tickets I got here as a student?"

TED GREEN, former Edmonton Oilers hockey coach, after receiving an injury report when rookie center **SHAUN VAN ALLEN** suffered a severe concussion. "He'll be fine," Green was told, "but he doesn't know who he is." "Good," Green responded, "tell him he's **WAYNE GRETZKY**."

HARRY NEALE, former Vancouver Canucks hockey coach: "Last season we couldn't win at home, and we were losing on the road. My failure as a coach was that I couldn't think of anyplace else to play."

Philadelphia Flyers defenseman **JAY WELLS**, not happy about some of the suspensions handed out in the season, said: "(NHL Executive Vice President) **BRIAN O'NEILL** is out to lunch. You can print it." A Philadelphia writer called O'Neill's office for a comment. The secretary answering the call explained: "Sorry, Mr. O'Neill is out to lunch."

Agent **MICHAEL BARNETT**, promising that hockey great **WAYNE GRETZKY** won't try to join wife **JANET JONES** in films: "His interest in acting is commensurate with her desire to play left wing."

Edmonton Oilers hockey coach **GLEN SATHER**, denying that his dog, Bouvier Butch, is trained to attack sports writers: "He's only trained to attack dumb sports writers."

Toronto Maple Leaf goalie **MARK LaFOREST** summed up his fight with New Jersey Devils goalie **SEAN BURKE** at Toronto one night: "I told him to take his mask off, and he obliged. So I hit him." La Forest lost the fight but Toronto won the game.

From Edmonton Oilers co-coach **JOHN MUCKLER**, claiming the stick work in the NHL is tame compared with the old days in the American and Eastern Leagues: "I remember **LARRY ZEIDEL** and another guy breaking the shafts of their sticks in a fight. Then they threw the shafts at each other like spears."

Edmonton Oilers hockey coach **GLEN SATHER** on former Oiler **WAYNE GRETZKY**, now with the Los Angeles Kings: "He deserves Beverly Hills. When he's sitting around sipping mint juleps by his pool in February, when he's slumming in his $2.7 million house and driving his Rolls Royce, he'll be a great inspiration to everybody else. Everybody can see what can happen when you work hard and dedicate yourself."

GENE UBRIACO, when he was coach of the Pittsburgh Penguins hockey team: "You're paid to win. I understand that. Let's face it, anybody can get paid to lose."

Quebec Nordiques hockey coach **MICHAEL BERGERON**, after the Pittsburgh Penguins used **MARIO LEMIEUX** and **PAUL COFFEY** as point men on a power play, late in an 8–2 win over the Nordiques: "That's like a squeeze play in baseball when you're nine runs ahead in the ninth inning."

After the National Hockey League lockout ended, **NICK KYPREOS**, New York Rangers left wing was en route from his home in Canada to New York. U.S. Customs officials asked Kypreos if he had anything to declare. His answer, "No. The NHL owners took it all."

MIKE DOWNEY of the Los Angeles *Times* was wondering how many people from Toronto and Montreal were living in Southern California. It's hard to say, but it recalled **JACK KENT COOKE'S** classic line when asked why his Los Angeles Kings hockey team wasn't drawing better at the Forum. "There are 800,000 Canadians living in the Los Angeles area," said Cooke, "and I've discovered why they left Canada. They hate hockey."

DONNIE POOLE is a journeyman fighter whose claim to fame is that the Washington Capitols once hired him to "instruct" their hockey players during training camp. Poole told Tony Kornheiser of the Washington *Post* that player response was varied. Michael Pivonka, for instance, fresh from Czechoslovakia, where fighting on the ice is forbidden, couldn't even make a fist. Dwight Schofield was so willing a student that he immediately challenged Poole to a fight. Schofield, one of the few Capitols who did not figure to need instruction, is 6'3" and 195 pounds, compared with Poole, who is 5'5" and 150. Schofield was known as the resident goon. "I agreed to fight him," Poole said. "He was all prepared for it. He had headgear, boots, and a cup. I had nothing. I said, 'I'll box you, but just don't hit me in the mouth, because I don't have a mouthpiece.'" Schofield's first punch was to Poole's mouth. Poole ducked, came up with a left hook, and knocked Schofield cold. Schofield was traded a week later.

From **BRIAN BURKE**, director of hockey operations for the then-struggling Vancouver Canucks of the National Hockey League: "The situation we're in reminds me of what **LOU VARIO** said a few years ago in New Jersey: 'I can see a light at the end of the tunnel but the tunnel goes to Europe.'"

Said Edmonton Oilers coach **GLEN SATHER**, responding to reports that the Oilers were having difficulty filling the stands since trading **WAYNE GRETZKY** to the Los Angeles Kings: "We've had 97 percent and 98 percent capacity. I'd have used 99 (Gretzky's uniform number), but we're not using that number any more."

Hockey great **GORDIE HOWE** recalls that when he set the National Hockey League scoring record, no one noticed. A week went by before a sportswriter thought to check on the record and discovered that Howe had long since broken it. But when Howe set the record for goals, there was a countdown—a long countdown. It took him forever to get the record goal. "They had put a bunch of blown-up balloons, ready to let loose in the celebration when I broke the record," Howe said. "By the time I got the record goal, all the air was coming out of the balloons, and they flopped around like a bunch of pigeons let loose."

SERGE SAVARD, Montreal Canadians All-Star defense-man, after a game against another All-Star, Detroit Red Wings **GORDIE HOWE**: "He didn't show me anything new. All of our guys have been playing like fifty-one year olds this season."

CHICO RESCH, the New York Islanders loquacious goal-tender: "If I wasn't talking, I wouldn't know what to say."

TOMMIE McVIE, coach of the Winnipeg Jets, on the improved play of the Buffalo Sabers: "They've got the same people as last year, but not the same players."

RAY FITZGERALD Boston *Globe* hockey columnist, on the thirty-three days it took National Hockey League president **JOHN ZIEGLER** to suspend three Boston Bruins for brawling with fans at

Madison square Garden: "He couldn't decide whether the 'I' came before or after the 'E' in **TERRY O'REILLY's** name."

FLOYD SMITH, NHL Toronto Maple Leaf coach, after his team was tied by the Edmonton Oilers: "I have nothing to say, and I'm only going to say it once."

GORDIE HOWE, fifty-one, playing out his career with the Hartford Whalers, following the debut of new teammate, **BOBBY HULL**, age forty-one: "The kid looked good in his first game."

BILL TORREY, New York Islander general manager, on scoring sensation **MIKE BOSSEY's** new contract: "I'm going to break with tradition to give you the details. It's a multi-year contract and for more money than I wanted to pay."

TERRY CRISP, Tampa Bay hockey coach, following an embarrassing 10–0 loss to Calgary: "I felt like General Custer at Big Horn. The only difference is that Custer didn't have to look at the game films of his massacre."

PART 7

TENNIS

A Brief History

Tennis, an indoor or outdoor game, is played on a rectangular court by two persons (singles) or four persons (doubles), who use rackets to hit a ball back and forth over a net. The object is to score points by striking the ball in such a way that an opponent cannot return it successfully.

Tennis, which originated in England, is popular among persons of all ages, male and female, with millions of participants. A tennis court measures seventy-eight feet long at the side lines and for the singles games, twenty-seven feet wide at the base lines. For doubles the court is made nine feet wider by extending the base lines four and a half feet in each direction. These extensions, enclosed by added sidelines, are called alleys.

A net parallel to the base lines divides the court at the center. Any of several court surfaces may be used, including grass, clay, concrete, wood, and synthetic fibers. The tennis ball is a cloth-covered rubber sphere that is white or yellow in color, approximately two and a half inches in diameter and two ounces in weight. Rackets of wood, the original material, are no longer popular and have been replaced by first steel and, of late, compositions such as aluminum, graphite, and fiberglass.

Tennis was first played in the United States in 1874 although opinions differ on who introduced it. Some of the game's most popular players over the years were Bill Tilden, Rod Laver, Don Budge, Jimmy Connors, Suzanne Lenglin, Billie Jean King, Martina Navratilova, and Chris Evert.

TENNIS

Tennis star **JIMMY CONNORS**, on experience: "The problem is that when you get it, you're too damned old to do anything about it."

Tennis Pro **JOHN McENROE**, to a heckler at a players championship tournament: "Do you have any problems other than that you're unemployed, and a moron, and a dork?"

DON BUDGE, on the new Ellsworth Vines and Gene Vier book, *Tennis: Myth and Method*, in which Vines picks Budge as the greatest tennis player of all time: "It's one of the most knowledgeable tennis books ever written."

Former tennis great **BILLIE JEAN KING:** "Tennis is a perfect combination of violent action taking place in an atmosphere of total tranquillity."

JEANNE AUSTIN, mother of sixteen year old tennis star **TRACY**: "When Tracy was eight, she would beat the best ladies at the tennis club in California and then go over to the baby-sitting area and play in the sandbox."

TV columnist **PRENTES ROGERS** caught ESPN's **CLIFF DRYSDALE** in an unfortunate use of words. Said Drysdale of tennis star **JIMMY CONNORS'** fondness for the clay courts at the French Open: "He loves to come to this surface and expose himself."

Tennis star **BORIS BECKER**, claiming he wasn't discouraged by his loss to **PAT CASH** in Australia: "I'm happy with my form. I'm starting to play like I did in my old days." Becker was nineteen when he made the statement.

There was never much love lost between tennis stars **JOHN McENROE** and **IVAN LENDL**. Lendl, a native of Czechoslovakia, was seeking U.S. citizenship and had expressed interest in playing on the U.S. Davis Cup team in the future. That prospect did not enthuse McEnnroe, a U.S. Davis Cup veteran. "That would be difficult for me to swallow at this point," McEnroe said when asked whether he would like to play on the same side as Lendl, his arch-rival for the number one ranking in tennis during the mid-1980s. Lendl, who like McEnroe was a consistent tour winner, fired back at McEnroe, saying that, "With his mouth, it's hard to imagine him having difficulty swallowing anything."

PART 8

OTHER SPORTS

OTHER SPORTS

DON CARTER, professional bowler: "One of the advantages of bowling over golf is that you very seldom ever lose a bowling ball."

Comedian **MILTON BERLE** on his new exercise program: "My doctor recently told me that jogging could add years to my life. I think he was right. I feel ten years older already."

KARL KREMSER, one-time Miami Dolphins place-kicker, on why he quit coaching soccer at Davidson College: "I thought the school had a commitment to soccer, but that wasn't the case—its emphasis was on academics."

Atlanta Braves owner **TED TURNER,** predicting success for his twenty-four hour TV news network: "We're going to be on the air until the end of the world. Then we'll play 'Nearer My God to Thee' and sign off."

MICHAEL LOURIE, French National sprint coach, asked why his country hasn't been able to produce great track and field teams the way it produces great wines: "Perhaps it is precisely because of our great wines that we have not had great track teams."

LARRY GUEST of the Orlando *Sentinel* at the end of his MAILBAG column, added this advisory: "Letters will not be considered if they are unsigned, longer than my attention span, or contain explosive devices."

BILL HALL, Montana hunting guide, on killing a grizzly bear in a protected area for endangered species: "When I saw that bear coming at me full steam, I didn't have any trouble deciding who was the endangered species."

Denver Broncos quarterback **JOHN ELWAY,** who played one summer in the New York Yankees organization, on the combined football and baseball careers of **BO JACKSON**: "I can't imagine making all that money and not having time to spend it."

DICK VITALE, popular basketball announcer, about his commentary style: "I should meet with Gorbachev because we have something in common—neither one of us can speak English."

ALLISON ROE of New Zealand, on why she runs the marathon: "I'm too slow to run anything else."

CHRIS CORCHIANI, North Carolina State basketball player, to ESPN announcer **DICK VITALE**, after the shiny-pated Vitale suggested Corchiani meet Vitale's eighteen year old daughter, Terri: "Mr. Vitale, does she have hair?"

YOGI BERRA, New York Yankees Hall of Famer:
"I really didn't say everything I said."
"When you come to the fork in the road, take it."
"I don't want to make the wrong mistake."

BENNY RICARDO, a former Minnesota Viking kicker and now a night club comedian, on baseball players: "They're not the smartest people in the world. They have a diamond diagramming where they have to go. And they still have to have coaches on first and third telling them which way to go, otherwise those guys would run all the way to the outfield warning track."

Supreme Court Justice **TOM CLARK**: "I'm convinced that every boy, in his heart, would rather steal second base than an automobile."

Former Giants outfielder **BILLY NORTH**: "Young horse runs fast, old horse knows the way."

Famous baseball great pitcher **SATCHEL PAIGE**: "Age is a question of mind over matter. If you don't mind, age don't matter."

Former President **GERALD FORD**: "I had pro offers from the Green Bay Packers and Detroit Lions, who were pretty hard up for linemen in those days. If I had gone into professional football, the name Jerry Ford might have been a household name today."

A great deal had been written about the possible move of the Chicago White Sox, but **MARY FRANCIS VEECK**, widow of former owner **BILL VEECK**, said, "For the past five years, I have been saying privately that the real movers and shakers in this town couldn't care less whether the Sox stay or go. I think Chicago is happy with the Bears, the Cubs, and **MICHAEL JORDAN**."

CASEY STENGEL: "Old timers weekends and airplane landings are alike. If you can walk away from them, they're successful."

CHARLES W. ELIOT, Harvard president: "This year I'm told our baseball team did well because one of our pitchers had a fine curve ball. I understand that a curve ball is thrown with a deliberate attempt to deceive. Surely that is not an ability we should want to foster at Harvard."

JOHN MOONEY, Salt Lake City *Tribune* sports editor: "If a doctor warns you that you have to watch your drinking, find a bar with a mirror."

Jockey **CHRIS McCARRON**, asked if he was nervous before riding Alysheba to victory in the Preakness: "Does Dolly Parton sleep on her back?"

Horse trainer **WAYNE LUKAS**, unimpressed when told that Alysheba trainer **JACK VAN BERG** would be wearing the same brown suit for the Preakness that he wore for the Kentucky Derby: "That's the only suit he's got."

PAUL GUANZON, Honolulu sportscaster, asked on a radio talk show how one becomes a sports announcer: "It's not politics, it's just who you know."

DR. HENRY WINKLER, University of Cincinnati President, who ended a much publicized search by appointing **MIKE McGEE** as his school's athletic director: "I'm tempted to call a press conference and announce our new librarian, who is much more important to the university."

Washington *Post's* **TONY KORNHEISER**, writing about diminutive Olympic swimmer **JANET EVANS**, after she had won the 400-meter freestyle: "She's so small, it's as if the wake from the other lanes should wash her onto the deck."

MYRTLE KRAMER, mother of football Hall of Famer **JERRY KRAMER** of the Green Bay Packers, before his book, *Instant Replay*, was published: "Don't use any words **ROY ROGERS** wouldn't use."

From **BILL "SPACEMAN" LEE**, former major league left-handed pitcher, who is living in northern Vermont: "How cold is it? It's so cold that the ice feels warm compared to the air."

After **SPUDS McKENZIE**, the "The Original Party Animal" of beer commercial fame, visited the Oakland-Alameda County

Coliseum for a promotion during an A's-Yankee game, New York's
RON KITTLE concluded: "Spuds is a better interview than **RICKY
HENDERSON.**"

Portland, Oregon, radio station KKEX had run a fake commercial for **SHAWN ECKHARDT'S** Professional Bodyguard School.
Among the classes offered: "Overnight Surveillance: "How many Big
Macs are enough?"

Former NFL running back and TV announcer **FRANK GIF-
FORD** on **HOWARD COSELL**, once a budding lawyer: "I asked him
to represent me in court on a parking violation, and they brought in a
manslaughter conviction."

It wasn't often that anyone succeeded in silencing boxer
MUHAMMAD ALI, but a quick-witted airline stewardess accomplished just that at the start of a flight from Washington D.C. to New
York. Stewardess: "Mr. Ali, please fasten your seat belt." Ali:
"Superman don't need no seat belt." Stewardess: "Superman don't
need no plane either."

JOHN STEIGERWALD in the Pittsburgh *Post-Gazette*:
"The fact that more Americans would rather watch bowling than
hockey says a lot more about Americans than it does about hockey."

Novelist **TOM CLANCY**, on his push to gain support for an
NFL expansion franchise in Baltimore at the 1992 owners meeting: "I
make $12 million a year, and I'm working the lobby like some cheap
hooker."

Basketball coach **GEORGE RAVELING** on sports writers:
"The best years of their lives are spent in the third grade."

BOB BEAMON, one of America's great track and field stars,
asked if he still thinks about the day in Mexico City when he set the
long jump records, replied: "Every day of my life."

JACK VAN BERG, trainer of the Kentucky Derby winner
Alysheba, was hoping to repeat in the Preakness in Baltimore, a
race he had won with Gate Dancer in 1984. "I'm staying at the same
motel where I stayed then," he said. "My wife said she wanted to try
this other motel, and I told her. 'You can go stay over there by yourself. I know where I'm staying.'" Van Berg also asked for the same
stall. "It's not that I'm superstitious, but that's what I'm doing."

DAVID PETERSON, a thirteen-year-old who is a five-time national scholastic chess champion, has played against many adults. The youngster from Chandler, Arizona, has found the experience both maddening and rewarding. Said Peterson, "Sometimes after you beat them, they still don't like you simply because you're a kid and you're annoying."

CARL LEWIS, assessing his impact on track and field events, told Tony Kornheiser of the Washington *Post*: "**BOB BEAMON** was forgotten. Who cared? I brought the event (long jump) back. No one cared about Bob Beamon until 1984. No one remembered Jesse Owens." Said Kornheiser: "You sit there thinking if Lewis applauds himself any harder, his hands will fall off."

Comedian **ALAN KING**: "One of the quickest ways to meet new people is to pick up the wrong ball on a golf course."

BRUCE JENNER, decathlon champion, on the difference between him and football great **JOE NAMATH**: "I spent twelve years training for a career that was over in a week. Joe spent a week training for a career that lasted twelve years."

CLEBURNE PRICE, Texas track coach, on Olympic sprinter **JOHNNY "LAM" JONES'** not running for the Texas track team: "It won't hurt us anymore than it would hurt a football team to lose **EARL CAMPBELL**."

ISSAC STERN, violinist, apologizing to the audience for his late arrival at a Sunday concert in Chicago Orchestra Hall: "I was competing with all those Bears football fans for a taxi. Had my name been **WALTER PAYTON**, I'd have had no trouble."

RED SMITH, the New York *Times'* sports columnist, on what he intended to do about the fact that his editor had killed a column in which he urged that the U.S. boycott the Olympics: "I'll write about the infield fly rule."

JEAN CRUGHET, French-born jockey: "When I first came here I worked around the Florida tracks. It's hard to learn English when everybody is speaking Spanish."

DANNY MASSH a Cambridge, Maryland, gas station attendant, midway through an unsuccessful attempt to swallow a world-record fifty-one raw eggs in an hour: "This is bad, man. Give me some water."

HERB STEVENS, trainer of Blue Grass winner **ROCKHILL NATIVE**, on assertions that his horse is too small to win the Kentucky Derby: "If size meant everything, a cow could beat a rabbit."

JIM HENSON, creator of the Muppets, attending homecoming festivities at his alma mater, Maryland ('60), without Miss Piggy: "She heard they were kicking around a pigskin and that all those people were eating hot dogs. She thought the whole thing was sort of barbaric."

TERRY KELLEHER, Everett (Washington) *Herald* TV columnist, on **JOHN McENROE's** claim that **JOHN LLOYD** is more popular than he is because Lloyd is married to **CHRIS EVERT**: "McEnroe wouldn't be popular if he were married to Marie Osmond."

Senator **WILLIAM PROXMIRE** (D., Wisconsin), who has been distributing his Golden Fleece awards to perpetrators of what he considers government waste, after giving one to the Interior Department for putting a $145,000 wave-making machine in the Salt Lake City community swimming pool: "It can be said that for the first time federal bureaucrats are making waves. In the meantime, the taxpayers are getting soaked."

JOHNNY WALKER, world middleweight wrist-wrestling champion, expounding on the demands of his sport: "It's about 90 percent strength and 40 percent technique."

ELEANOR HOLM, a gold medalist in swimming at the 1932 Olympic Games, when asked by the Washington *Post's* Jane Leavy about an Olympic boycott: "I want to tell you something, hon. I'd think twice about going to Russia. Of course it's easy for me to say, an old broad who's had her day."

The Golden Oldies international rugby tournament in Toronto required that players be at least thirty-five. Players over seventy wear purple or gold shorts and cannot be tackled. "The Japanese know how to use that rule," said one of the organizers, surgeon **CAM MacARTHUR**. "They pack their sides with very nimble over-seventies. But we know how to deal with that. We just lie down and let them trip over us."

Chicago Cubs broadcaster **HARRY CARAY**, in *Sport* magazine, on rumors that he was fired by the St. Louis Cardinals in 1969 because he had had an affair with the much younger wife of a brewery executive: "If you were me, would you go around denying rumors like that?"

BILL LYON of the Philadelphia *Inquirer*: "Statistics can be used to support anything, including statisticians."

According to police, about a mile into the Clearwater (Florida) *Sun's* 10,000-meter road race, one of the 1,200 runners left the course and entered a nearby convenience store. There he grabbed $34 from the cash register and fled on foot, unsuccessfully pursued in a very different kind of race by cops summoned by a store employee. Said one officer: "He simply outran us."

MICHAEL JACKSON, one of the stars of the World Track and Field Championships in Stuttgart, Germany, on the $28,000 Mercedes given to each gold medalist: "Anybody good enough to win one, already has one."

HOWARD SCHENKEN, who died in 1987 at the age of seventy-five, was widely regarded as the greatest bridge player in the world, as the following, perhaps apocryphal, exchange between two tournament players attest:
"If you had to play a match for your life, whom would you choose as a partner?"
"Howard Schenken."
"And if Schenken wasn't available?"
"I'd wait until he was."

Among the stories they tell about **BOB WATERS**, popular *Newsday* boxing writer who died recently, is the one about the lost wallet. A group of writers were sitting in the Galleria Lounge in Caesars Palace in Las Vegas, Nevada, when they overheard the bartender say that a wallet had been found the previous night. "That must be mine," Waters said. "Just a minute," the bartender said, "I think there's a name inside. What's your name?" "Genuine Leather," replied Waters.

LARRY GUEST of the Orlando *Sentinel* recalled that a top editor of the Dallas *Morning News* once banned the use of nicknames such as Tommy, Charlie, etc. Wrote Guest: "A football writer promptly reported that 'Doak Walker had been sidelined by a Charles Horse.'"

From Hall of Fame baseball announcer **HARRY CARAY**: "I never realized how short a month is until I started paying alimony."

From former Washington Redskin kicker **JESS ATKINSON**, whose father was a Navy pilot: "I told him that when I was playing football at the University of Maryland, I made ninety-three straight extra points before missing one. He said, 'Well Jess, I had 104 successful night carrier landings. What do you think would have happened if I only had ninety-three?' I stopped talking."

Announcer **GARY BENDER** asked **AKEEM OLAJUWON**, giant star of the Houston Rockets, if there was any sport he had not mastered. "I can't swim," Olajuwon said. Said Bender, "Well, neither can I." "Yeah," said Olajuwon, "but I can wade out a lot farther than you."

The subject was academics, and Illinois basketball coach **LOU HENSON**, who attended Okay (Oklahoma) High School, said: "There were thirteen in my graduating class, so I can safely say I was in the top 10 percent. As a matter of fact, I've gone up to number one because five or six years ago the school burned and all the records went with it."

From **BILL LYON** of the Philadelphia *Inquirer*: "The advantage of being a celebrity is that when you bore people they feel it's their fault."

From **CHRIS BERMAN** ESPN's dispenser of outrageous nicknames: Greg (Life Is a) Cadaret."

Horse racing thoroughbred owner **STEVE SHAPIRO'S** proposal to **KAREN KIRCHER** on the Santa Anita tote board Valentine's Day began, "Karen—let's become an entry."

SKIP CARAY, announcer for the Atlanta Hawks and Atlanta Braves: "If a young guy asked me for advise on how to get into broadcasting, I'd say: 'Hit .350 or win the Heisman Trophy.'"

San Francisco 49er linebacker **TOM COUSINEAU**, to a reporter who asked him if he majored in basket-weaving at Ohio State: "No, something much simpler, journalism."

TOMMY JOHN, outstanding left handed pitcher, at age forty-four, asking writers to try to avoid references to his age in stories: "My wife doesn't like it. She says everyone thinks she's also forty-four."

EDDIE "THE EAGLE" EDWARDS, also known as **"FAST EDDIE,"** was a British ski jumper who became a cult hero at the Winter Olympics. Eddie doesn't soar, he plummets. He finished fifty-eighth and last in the seventy meter event with a jump of 179 feet. The winner went 293 feet. No matter. The crowd loved him. Edward's parents flew from Britain to watch their son, a twenty-four year old plasterer who has been jumping for only two years. "I thought about waving to them while I was on the jump," he said, "but I was too busy trying to stand up to do it."

SALVATORE VARRIALE runs the Parma Angels Gestione Baseball Club. He also hosts the Italian version of **MEL ALLEN'S** "This Week in Baseball: "We have very good ratings," says Varriale during a visit to the Toronto Blue Jays training camp. "Of course we have a pretty good lead-in audience. Our show is on at 12:30 P.M. on the same station as the Pope's weekly half-hour program, which begins at noon."

U.S. synchronized swimming coach **GAIL EMERY**, responding to a suggestion that her sport is more theater than athletics: "We basically have come from the **ESTHER WILLIAMS** water ballet era to a full-fledged athletic sport. Try running a five-minute mile and holding your breath for two-thirds of it."

Australian Rules Football official **ROSS OAKLEY**, promising that fans will enjoy an exhibition game that was scheduled at the Los Angeles Coliseum: "Even those who don't understand it should get a real buzz out of it. Some have described the game as one of organized mayhem. I think that's unfair. There's nothing organized about it."

JIM SUNDBERG of the Chicago Cubs, asked about a near miss with another plane during a team flight: "I don't know how close it was, but the lady in 13D was having the chicken dinner."

New York Mets executive **ED LYNCH**: "There's something about **NANCY KERRIGAN** that reminds me of **RYNE SANDBERG**, and something about **TONYA HARDING** that reminds me of **LENNY DYKSTRA**."